STACE

Stronger
THAN
BROKEN

One couple's decision to move through an affair

Copyright ©2014 by Stacey Greene

All rights reserved. No part of this book may be reproduced, stored in a retrieval system, or transmitted in any form or by any means – electronic, mechanical, photocopy, recording or any other – without permission in writing from the author.

All Scripture quotations are taken from The Holy Bible, New International Version Copyright © 1973, 1978, 1984 by International Bible Society.

Printed in the United States of America
ISBN: 978-0-9904092-0-5
LCCN: 2015913801

*To all of the men and women who still
think marriage is sacred and
worth fighting for.*

*Although the names and some of the situations
have been changed slightly to protect my family,
please know that the pain of infidelity
is real and not to be taken lightly.*

*May this book remind all married couples to
cherish, respect and honor the vows
you made and carry forgiveness
in your heart.*

God Bless You.

Contents

Introduction vii

1. How It All Began 1
2. The Nasty Text 7
3. Broken 13
4. Faking It 17
5. My Ignorance 23
6. 408 29
7. The Poignant Sermon 41
8. My Assignment 47
9. Research 55
10. Songs 61
11. The Funeral 67
12. In Person 73
13. Loyalty 79
14. The Extent of It 83

15.	Convicted	93
16.	Fairy Tales Do End	101
17.	The Phone Call	111
18.	Lessons in Love	119
19.	Jazz Night	127
20.	Jealousy	133
21.	Summertime	141
22.	Our Anniversary	149
23.	The Holidays	157
24.	Stronger Than Broken	167

Introduction

My intent of sharing my pain is to catch couples before one or both of them break Commandment No. 7. No person should ever feel broken, split in two, fragmented, confused or lost in a relationship that they thought was just fine. I do not profess to be a psychologist, counselor or expert in relationships. I am just like many of you, trying to juggle the demands of motherhood, career, daughter and wife.

In this day and age when frenetic activity and instant gratification are the norm, it is almost counterculture to stop and assess the stress that a busy lifestyle can cause. It is so much easier for couples to throw away the marriage like an old pair of running shoes, when things get difficult, and then they blame it on each other for their own unhappiness. I thought my husband and I were normal—whatever that might mean. I now know that there is no "normal." Each couple must stop and smell the roses once in a while. Each relationship needs a makeover every now and then. Spouses can learn from each other and continue to grow together as a couple if each one is willing to share in the other's life.

Take this opportunity to look at your spouse as someone worth reinvesting in and worth growing old with. Remember the good old memories, but be sure to make some brand new ones as well. Remember that your children will look to you to set an example for the kinds of things they will look for and expect in their own relationships. Leave a legacy that you can be proud of.

CHAPTER ONE

How It All Began

> "Lovers forever, face to face
> My city or mountains
> Stay with me, stay"
>
> **Leather and Lace**
> —Stevie Nicks

My husband and I met at a restaurant back in the '80s. I was really not looking for romance. I was still fairly hurt from a relationship that had broken up after four years. Yes, I had the few transitional boyfriends, but nothing like the breakup that was still haunting me. One night when my friend Judy and I were out to eat, I overheard a handsome man asking the waitress if there were any vegetarian items on the menu. Being a vegetarian myself, I knew I just had to go over and talk to him. I found out that he and I grew up in the same neighborhood and I ran cross-country with one of his sisters when I was in high school. Fast forward to the next year. We were already living together, and picking out races to do together. We were both avid runners and loved to compete.

We married, and a few years later the kids started coming. First we had the twins, Robbie and Richie, then two years later Theo followed, then Grace three years after that. Three boys and one girl in just under seven years takes a toll on the body, the romance and the time we had for each other. Still, we always enjoyed squeezing in great sex and an occasional run in the state park. Jim took the twins in the double stroller while I took the little ones in the double baby jogger. We were quite a sight out on the jogging trails!

Complications started in the late '90s when my father became ill with Alzheimer's disease and Jim's mother had her first of three heart attacks. The kids were all into sports and clubs. We began playing a well-orchestrated game of tag team. One of us would take the twins to soccer practice while the other would pick up the younger ones from swimming. One of us would make dinner while the other was taking a trip to one of the aging parents' houses to check on things. Our trail runs became a thing of the past as we began "running" the kids here and there, trying to see each band concert, game played, swim meet or award that was presented.

We started arguing a bit more about everything from finances to groceries, kids' needs to his needs, my free time versus his free time. There was even a short period of time when we left each other nasty notes, just so that we did not have to talk to each other face-to-face. This was not often, but still very hurtful and unhealthy.

Date nights became rare and I noticed that our taste in music, friends and other activities had shifted dramatically. Jim had his male friends from work, and I had a whole slew of mommy friends from playgroups, school functions and the like. Jim started having dinner in the basement in his "man cave" and I started watching shows with no redeeming value in the family room. We still went out to eat from time to time, but generally found something to argue about on our date. I even remember one night at a local dive when I got up and walked out halfway through the meal. I started walking home and was at least a mile out before Jim drove by and made me get in the car. I guess he had to finish his meal and pay the bill before coming to find me walking home in the dark!

As the kids got older, they spent time on the computer, played video games between practices, did their homework and generally left us alone. They began to have their own friends and if their homework was done, they were allowed to go out on the weekends.

Even our sleeping arrangements became dysfunctional. During the years that I nursed the children, I ended up sleeping in their rooms so often that when they were weaned, Jim said he had grown used to sleeping alone. He became a very light sleeper, and I noticed that when I slept in *our* bed, he was crabby and irritable the next day. Jim used every excuse, from my tossing and turning too much, to waking him when I got up to pee, and even that the mattress dipped down too much when our bodies were too close to each other. It just seemed easier to keep the family peace if I slept on the couch in the living room or the futon in the family room. He had convinced me that it was totally normal for us to be incompatible sleep partners. We would still have our conjugal visits, then I would retire to the futon.

I knew that somewhere in that arrangement we still loved each other, but he seldom said the actual words that every woman needs to hear. When I would tell him I loved him, he would usually respond with "I know," or a quick "I love you too," which sounded like one long word: "Iloveyoutoo," because he said it so fast, under his breath.

After the twins graduated from high school, Robbie chose to stay in state, but far enough away to live in a dorm, and Richie moved out of state. It was strange to see them go, and even more unusual to see such a close-knit pair choose colleges away from each other. Still, we had to pat ourselves on the back for raising independent boys with decent grades and minds of their own.

As our 25th anniversary approached, I thought we should renew our vows. I was so proud of us. How many married couples in this day and age even make it to 25 years? Jim went along with the idea, but not being a big church-goer, he just wanted to have a simple "to-do" at the house with some friends. We made the preparations. We spared no expense and had a sheet cake, balloons, real invitations sent through the snail mail, and for the first time we catered the food. What a relief to have delicious food as well as a fairly sunny day to throw such a gala. Richie was the only one not able to make it up from school, but Robbie came, as well as my mother and both of Jim's folks. The pastor arrived and after greeting our friends, he began the vows.

I was thrilled that when it came time to kiss the bride, my typically shy and reserved husband laid a sexy kiss on me that made me blush. It lasted a whole lot longer than the kiss on our first wedding day. The whole evening I was on cloud nine because he had such a silly grin on his face and had given me such a fantastic kiss in front of everyone. I had it made. And now being down to just two kids at home, I knew we would have even more time to reconstruct our marriage.

Shortly after the party, Theo began to drive. Grace was almost 14 and able to stay alone if Theo was out with friends. I started bugging Jim about going out again, but I really didn't like going to the bars that Jim favored, and he really didn't like the Thai food and "chick flicks" that I preferred. A few times he had promised to take me out, but somehow we just ended up on the couch, while Jim drank a few beers as we watched a movie.

"I thought we were going out tonight," I said, as Jim cracked open a beer and reached for the remote.

"I dunno. Let's see what's on TV," was his response.

"But this is one of the last weekends I have off before I start my holiday retail job. I'll go wherever you want," I offered.

"Oh, look. There's an old Clint Eastwood movie on," he said, without losing eye contact with the boob tube. That was it. End of discussion. We sat on the couch like we had a thousand other times and watched a movie.

Still, I thought we were doing well. I prayed prayers of gratitude about him almost every day and strategically placed love notes all over the house where I knew he would find them. I was delighted at the fact that, even after all of the years gone by, Jim was still trying to come up with new material in the bedroom. He was always ready, willing and able. Don't get me wrong, he wasn't a freak and had never gone all "Fifty Shades of Grey" on me, but still, he liked to keep things interesting, and as a red-blooded, American woman, I appreciated that.

I began working until 11 in the evening from September through February as a way to bring in more income for the two sons we had in college. I knew Jim liked to go out with his friend Marcus, and I was OK with him having his guy time, as I knew how much I savor the occasional lunch date or girls night out. Couples need to have their own friends and keep their own identities. But when I went out with my friends, I always came home at a reasonable hour. Jim, on the other hand, stayed out late. Often I would come home from my retail job and turn on "Saturday Night Live," while waiting for him to come home and give me the goods. If he was later than 1 a.m., I would fall asleep on the couch until I heard the key in the door.

On weekday evenings and on Sunday afternoons we liked watching some of the same sitcom re-runs, so I purchased the first several seasons of "Mash" and "Cheers." Many a Sunday afternoon would go by under a blanket, laughing at the characters in the shows. The kids would also join in for the "Cheers" episodes and we would watch a few of their silly reality shows just to spend more time with them. One night I did not fall asleep in the family room and went up to our own bedroom to sleep. Imagine my total and complete surprise when I opened the door to see Jim quickly throw his cell phone under the sheet.

Proverb 10:9
The man of integrity walks securely, but he who takes crooked paths will be found out.

CHAPTER TWO
The Nasty Text

"Words like violence break the silence
Come crashing in into my little world
Painful to me, Pierce right through me"

Enjoy the Silence
—Depeche Mode

"What are you doing?" I asked. I laughed at first because Jim is not a technologically minded man, and rarely ever has his phone with him. Still, I went to grab it and it slipped. The battery flew out as the back fell off of the cheap, little, pay-as-you-go phone I made him get for emergencies.
"Give me my phone," he said.
"Why? You don't even use it," I replied.
"Give it to me."
"No."
"It's *my* phone," he snapped.
"So!" was the only pathetic thing I could think of to say, as my mind was putting it all together in slow motion.

Cogs in my brain turned like an elephant walking through molasses, and finally, stunned, I asked: "So who is she, and for how long?"

No response.

"*Who* is she and for *how long?*" I demanded.

"I don't want to talk about it. I'm going to bed," he replied.

I don't remember much of the conversation beyond that point. All the blood in my body rushed to my gut and I became light-headed. Even my arms and legs felt light, as if they were trying to float right off of my body. I remember being shocked, mad and then more shocked. I felt, of all of the things that *had* gone wrong in my life and of all of the things that *could* have gone wrong in my life, my marriage to Jim was always the constant. He was always my rock. He was my northern star. No way could this even be happening.

I finally got him to tell me that "it" had not been going on for more than four or five months, and that she was a 41-year-old single mom, never married, with a 3-year-old kid. He met her at a bar and they had an "instant connection." OK. Now that was where I should have vomited! I think the poor bastard had watched one too many episodes of "The Bachelor" with our daughter. If I ever hear *anyone* ever again say, "We had a connection," I will bitch-slap them. I have "connections" with people all the time, but that doesn't mean I go on dates with them, text them and then try to hide my phone.

I took the pieces of the phone with me to the family room downstairs and hid them. I knew Jim would not rest until he had the phone back, and sure as I know my husband, he came storming down less than a minute later, begging me not to put the phone back together.

"I hid it," was all I had to say as I pulled blankets onto the couch.

"Please," he begged.

I now used his line back at him: "I'm going to bed."

He retreated. I tried to sleep but could not. Around midnight I figured he was asleep, so I put the phone back together in the downstairs bathroom. After locking the door and with shaking hands I read a text about how she knew where she was going to take him Friday night (when I was working).

The next text read: *I wish we were there now, or in your pants.*

The reality of those words sent me to the floor. The anger came first as I furiously texted a reply: *the jig is up. it's the wife. you can have him!!*

The tears came next. Ah, the tears. I must have let Niagara fall that night. I had no idea how much water can flow from two little, brown eyes.

I hid the phone again and tried to go back to sleep. I must have dozed a bit, because when I awoke at 1 a.m., there was a two-page letter on my stomach, hand written by Jim. The handwriting was atrocious, so it took me a while to read all about how he hoped I didn't put the phone back together and throw away 25 years of marriage over his very selfish act.

"I know it was selfish and I tried to stop," it read. "It was all about feeling young again and it was addicting. I couldn't turn it off. I know it was wrong and selfish and she tried to stop too but we couldn't. Maybe you and I are better off apart. I don't know. You are always the one who puts more into the relationship than I do, and we both have been so lonely."

It went on and on, and the more I read, the more confused I became. Lonely? After I had been begging for date nights and more quality time? Lonely? After that sloppy kiss and goofy smile at our anniversary party just months before? Feeling young? Aren't we both still screwing like people in their 20s? Heck, now that the kids are older and there is less running around to do, I had even gotten myself back in shape and was running on the treadmill and lifting weights in our basement. Working my holiday retail job was also bringing in new and youthful clothing for Jim, who had never lost the rock-solid body I married years ago. To top that off, if he wanted to feel young again, why did he find a lady in her 40s with a kid? Why not a 20-year-old bimbo with big boobs for that jerk!

The next morning I went up to talk to him in the bedroom and he startled me. He was actually just propped up against the hallway wall, in the dark, looking like he had been through hell and back. Could it be that he felt bad about all of this? Why was he just standing there? We went into the bedroom and I faked that I could not read his handwriting. I made the son of a bitch read it out loud to me. Jim sat on the edge of the bed while I stood at his side. He placed his head against my chest and I placed one arm around his shoulder. He read the whole two pages, word for word, with a crackly voice, as if he may have even been stifling the tears.

Still standing, I put my other arm around his shoulders and drew him in even closer. I am not sure why. I am sure many a scorned woman would have attacked their man with both fists firing. Perhaps I felt such a need to *be* consoled that I decided to console *him* instead. The top of his head smelled wonderful as I breathed him in. None of this made any sense. Too many emotions were bombarding me all at once. After several minutes of just soaking in the reality of the letter all over again, Jim gently removed my arms and announced that he had to get ready for work.

I followed him downstairs and began washing the last-night's dishes while he made his usual brown bag lunch of an apple, a cheese sandwich, a protein bar and some cookies. I got the cereal and milk for him and tried to do the same things I usually do for him every day. Maybe if I acted normal, this would all go away.

As Jim grabbed his car keys from the hook on the wall, he noticed that I had not gotten my bowl out to eat. Who could eat? My whole body had shut down. I was basically a walking corpse, just going through the motions for Theo and Gracie, who had just bounced downstairs oblivious to anything unusual. Later that morning, Jim called from work. He never does. I guess guilt can be a wonderful thing. He wanted to make sure I ate something, but instead of eating, I got on the treadmill, punched some hard rock into the radio dial and set the speed to the fastest setting I could manage.

2 Corinthians 12:9
But he said to me, "My grace is sufficient for you, for my power is made perfect in weakness."
Therefore I will boast all the more gladly about my weaknesses, so that Christ's power may rest on me.

CHAPTER THREE
Broken

"I don't wanna be here anymore. I wanna be somewhere else normal and free like I used to be"

Big White Room
—*Jessie J.*

With sweat still dripping down my face, I shut the music and the treadmill off and went back into the kitchen for some water. With the kids now at school and Jim at work I decided to write down the words that were flashing in my brain during the last part of my run. Words. Just words. As I wrote, more words continued seeping into me like spilled juice onto a paper towel. Words that were saturating every cell. Words that would play over and over in my head for many months to follow.

    cheated on
    lied to
    fucked
    confused
    raped
    hurt

torn
bleeding
pissed on
slipping away
bent
wrecked
tormented
just a screw
betrayed
damaged goods
abused
beyond repair
misunderstood
beaten down
whored out
unloved
trash
uncherished
ugly
humiliated
false life
sad
pissed off
vulnerable
angry
unsure
scared
ruined
inferior
bitch
BROKEN

I contemplated starting a journal again. It had been a few years since I really kept one. Starting a journal would make me acknowledge my intense feelings, and that truly scared me. Writing individual words was one thing, but I feared that writing down all the details would make it too real.

When Jim returned home from work, and the kids were home from school, I dragged him upstairs and said, "We really need to figure this out!"

"I know. I'm just confused. I still want to see her," he said.

My head was spinning and there was that feeling in my gut again. I know, most people would say that the feeling was hunger pains from not eating all day, but any woman would know that it was that sick, catastrophic, all-consuming feeling that life will never, ever be the same again. I should have been impressed with the honesty he displayed admitting that he still wanted to see her, but naturally, it only served to twist and turn the knife he had already stabbed into my heart.

"Well, you can't have both," I snapped. I've never known anyone who can successfully ride two horses with one ass.

"We can play nice for another few years until Grace is out of high school, and then walk away. This will give us time to get out of debt a bit."

" ...Or we can fix this," I added.

I didn't really mean the comment about walking away, but the words were just flying out of my mouth before I could filter my thoughts. At the time, what else would suffice? He had just said he still wanted to see her.

"Maybe we should talk to someone," Jim suggested. I stared, stunned as this comment made me think he seemed to be leaning toward fixing this. I promised to set up an appointment with our pastor. Although my Jimmy is not a huge God fan, he had started to attend church more regularly when our church had changed pastors. The new guy really puts life into the sermons. He always keeps it real, while showing us how stuff that happened 2,000 years ago can still apply to the issues we all have today. Jim agreed that the pastor would be a good place to start.

"Should I set it up for any night this week?"

"Yeah... No, wait. Don't put it on a Tuesday. Doesn't Theo have his trombone thing?" Jim recalled.

"You're right, he has his tryout for the jazz band."

I cannot believe I forgot. For the last two years Theo has had an opportunity to travel with a small ensemble of high school students during spring break. It is quite an honor. Last year I went as one of the teachers' helpers, and I was blown away at his playing. Jim chose to stay home last year and take care of the other kids. Besides, staying home meant he did not have to take a personal day. I secretly hoped that Theo would not make the cut, so I would not have to leave my cheating husband at home while I was miles and miles away.

I called our church and left a message with the receptionist for the pastor to call me as soon as possible. I did not want to say any more, other than it was rather pressing and to please have him call my home or my cell phone.

Proverbs 12:22
The Lord detests lying lips, but he delights
in men who are truthful.

CHAPTER FOUR
Faking It

"Everything's so blurry and everyone's so fake and everybody's empty and everything is so messed up. Preoccupied without you I cannot live at all."

Blurry
—Puddle of Mudd

The next two days were much like the first. I awoke crying into my blanket, and Jim would hold me for as long as I needed. I faked being OK long enough to get Theo and Grace off to school, then when Jim left for work, I would go for an intense treadmill run with the most high-energy music on the CD player or radio that I could find. One of the favorites to run to was Lady Ga Ga's "Judas." She can't help but to love Judas even though he was the beginning of the end for Jesus. She forgives him when his tongue lies through his brain and she forgives him when she is betrayed. "I'm just a holy fool, Oh baby it's so cruel but I'm still in love with Judas baby." Is Jim the Judas in this song? Will I forgive him when his tongue lies through his brain?

I am not sure if I was running out the anger or the sadness. Both emotions were talking turns surging through my entire body. No amount of heavy breathing or sweat would make them leave me. Still unable to eat, I began running some apples and green foods through the juicer. I dug some vitamins out of the kitchen cupboard and popped a few of those as well. Appetite or no appetite, I was determined to stay somewhat functional for the kids, who still seemed oblivious to what issues mom and dad were having.

Jim called at lunchtime and asked if I had eaten anything. He seemed concerned that I might pass out on the treadmill. I sort of wish I had. Anything would be better than feeling like this. It would have been great to have Jim come home and see me lying on the floor. *He* did this to me. *He* broke me. *He* deserves all of the guilt, the shame and the torment.

Next on the list was to call the pastor again and get to work. People at work knew nothing, as I had stopped crying in the car and waited until I was in the parking lot to apply my make up. Only on day four of no solid foods, one of my co-workers mentioned that I looked slim, and wondered what I was doing. I shrugged it off but when she saw me drinking green juice at lunch I played that I was doing one of those silly juice cleanses. I couldn't wait to get out of that one, yet I knew I was going to explode keeping all of those emotions inside of me. I figured the only one I could really talk to was my sister in Arizona. I figured that if Jimmy could spend his pay-as-you-go phone money on texts to another woman, I could run up our land line a bit!

So, five full days after catching Jim texting, I mustered up the strength to call my sister. She had been through one divorce that was largely in part to *both* of them cheating on each other.

She was sympathetic and all, but somehow I felt she was distracted, so I kept our call short. She offered to pray for me, and I willingly took her up on the offer.

Back at home I made a great dinner for the family, and pushed the food around on my plate enough for the kids to assume I was eating. Jim knew I was not, and shot me glances of concern and possibly guilt. While washing dishes, he slid up to me from behind and slipped his strong arms around my waist. He pushed my hair over to the side and kissed the side of my neck gingerly. He whispered in my ear that he really would feel better if I ate a little bit. Not a chance. I loved the fact that he was concerned about *me* and not sneaking up to the bedroom to text *her*.

"What have you eaten today?" he queried.

"I put some stuff in the juicer," I replied.

"That's all?"

"Yep."

"Shelly, that's not enough, especially if you ran too. You ran too, didn't you?"

"Just a little," I lied.

"Why won't you eat?"

"My body won't let me. I just have no appetite so why should I bother?"

"It's not healthy."

"Well neither is thinking I had the perfect marriage and finding out my husband is sneaking around."

He had no reply to that, as Grace and Theo came in the kitchen together looking for some sort of desert.

"Mom, the coach said he wants me swimming the fly in the next meet! I hate the fly," said Grace as she picked up an empty cookie tin to shake it.

"He must think you can do it baby."

"Mom, you *know* I am a back-stroker. Hailey is our best flyer."

"Maybe he wants to give everyone a chance to perfect all of the strokes."

"Who knows? Can I have the rest of this ice cream?" she asked as she pulled out some vanilla from the freezer.

"Sure hon. I am going to bed early. I want to start a new book." I headed for the stairs. No futon or couch for me tonight.

Truthfully, I wanted to get on the computer in the bedroom and Google "cheating." I saw many websites as well as chat rooms for the people who have been cheated on. I hate chat rooms. I went on one for young parents when I had the twins, and it was so confusing keeping up with all of the various replies to my questions about potty training and nursing. Still, tonight I stumbled across one site that had a free e-book to download. It talked about not appearing so needy to your spouse. It is a real turn-off for them and may push them away further, it said. It also warned against asking a lot of questions about the affair. The most shocking thing that it said, several times, was to stop telling the cheater that you love him or her. What? The reasoning was that it would just confuse the poor sap. The cheating bastard (my words) will wonder if you are just saying you love them out of insecurity, out of guilting them into leaving the affair, or even make the cheater think, "How could you love me after what I did to you?"

Well crap! All of those things are very valid, but what if you are genuinely still in love with the sap? What if all of the above reasons are true, but you still can't help vomiting those words out on a daily basis? I don't think I have ever gone a single day without telling my husband that I love him. Even when we went through those stressful, nasty years when we were taking care of old parents and younger kids, I still let him know quite frequently that he was my love.

I made my decision to take everything I read on the Internet with a grain of salt. All of my new-age friends are always telling me to go with your gut. Right now my gut tells me to be truthful and honest and to show that I have always been here. I never left.

My friends that study the law of attraction are always telling me that you manifest what you think about most. What is it they say? "What you think about you bring about." Well, I'm not sure I have ever thought about Jimmy cheating on me. No, I'm sure I have never thought about it. Was Jim thinking on some level "affair"? Does this even have to do with me at all? Maybe Jim was manifesting unhappiness in some way and it came out as an excuse to look elsewhere. Is there some way on some level that we both brought this about? All of the questions, all of the self-blaming and all of the confusion was wearing me down. I wondered if sleeping in a warm, comfortable bed would help.

When Jim came into the room, I approached him with wanting to sleep in my own bed again.

"Hey, I was just thinking that I really want to try to sleep in here again." No answer.

"I know you say you can't get a good night's sleep, but what if I just came up here on the days when your schedule allows you to sleep in a bit, or I could try to sleep here until I have to wake to pee. Then I can go back downstairs," I added.

"I guess we could try." he replied.

"Thanks, Jimmy."

I slept with my husband for the whole night. I stayed as far on the other side of the bed as possible without falling off. I slept stiff as a board and tried not to move the sheets. I held my bladder until morning. I even tried to breathe softly. At one point his foot touched mine and it was a little slice of heaven. It brought back a flood of memories from our younger days when we made silly rules about what body parts could touch during sleeping hours. No bones on bones as being a slim man, he didn't want my knees poking him all night. To avoid this, when we would spoon each other, we would share a pillow between our knees and get as close as possible without being poked by elbows or knees. We used to play footsie before going to sleep and had these great competitions with our feet. I would put my foot on top of his and push down hard. He would flex his foot upward and see who had the stronger and longer hold before our calf muscles gave in. Then we switched and he would put his foot on top of mine. Now I just jumped when his foot accidentally brushed against mine. Where did we go? Can we ever get back?

2 Corinthians 5:7
We live by faith, not by sight.

CHAPTER FIVE
My Ignorance

"You abandoned me
Love don't live here anymore
Just a vacancy
Love don't live here anymore"

Love Don't Live Here Anymore
—Madonna

Friday came and I called my employer and made an excuse not to come in. I wanted to make sure Jim was on a date with *me* and not the *other* woman who wanted to be in his pants. We went to a movie at the second run theater. I kept trying to think about where we went and what we did on our last date together. I didn't have a clue where we went, what we did or even when we dated. Was it three months or four? I worked the retail job in the evenings from fall through winter when the store does inventory, so it must be about five or six months. Even before that, we barely went out alone. We did plenty of things with the kids, but did not share many opportunities to really relate to each other, one on one.

I think I was trying too hard to act normal. I faked laughs at the funny parts of the movie for about the first half. Jim doesn't know how to fake things, so I was genuinely thrilled when he not only laughed, but also made great eye contact with me several times. He even asked me if I wanted to get a beer afterward. Poor guy. Doesn't he remember that I don't like drinking? When I was young, I had my moments, but when I had decided to get serious about running and health, I put aside all of the useless calories and runaway sugars in alcohol. I was either pregnant or nursing for so long that, after about eight years straight of no alcohol, I just decided I really didn't need it.

Back at home we hung out with Theo and Grace while they finished watching a movie, then we retired to our room. We sat on the bed and started making out. Those soft kisses were killing me. One part of me was so turned on and ready for much more, while the other side of me wept bitterly. I told him that we could start things up, but I was not ready to do everything with him. He seemed to understand, so we continued to kiss for a while. I excused myself to go to the bathroom, but when I returned, I heard that little ring tone of Jim's, telling me a text came in on his phone. I heard it from the backpack he takes to work to carry his lunch and running clothes in.

Really? Seriously? I grabbed the cell from his bag and sure enough it was *her*, with a text that read: *u 2*.

"I just texted her to have a good night."

That's when it hit me that Jim and this *thing* truly had a relationship and not just a fling. I stood there stunned, with the feeling of being completely used. I was just a lay and the other half of the paycheck. I was just the mother of his kids. I was just the vessel he could use when not with her. I was blind and ignorant not to have seen this.

Before all of this happened, he never texted anyone. He always bitched that it cost him his pay-as-you-go minutes and if I needed to call him, I could always call his work number. I know that our kids have even tried to show him how to text and he's said it's just too much trouble to find his reading glasses and to press all of those tiny little buttons. Well, apparently *she* taught him how to text. The thought of some other woman leaning over his shoulder and placing her fingers on his to show him what buttons to press made me cringe.

"Go ahead and tell her to stop," he offered as he handed me the phone. I texted her to stop and said that it was me, the wife. Somehow that only made me feel more used and beaten down. I guess Jim was too gutless to do it himself. So the old ball-and-chain had to step in and tell them to stop. I felt like a mom telling two siblings to stop fighting. I can't believe he made me intervene for him. Coward!

Jim tried to make me feel better by giving me the phone and telling me, "Here, baby. I don't even need the phone. You can have it." You know damned well I took it! Logic told me that he could still call her or use a friend's phone from work or any number of ways to contact her if he really wanted to. Still, taking that phone made me feel some small bit of power in my otherwise powerless and out-of-control life.

Oh, God. It dawned on me that friends from his work must know about this. I know he goes out a lot with Marcus. Hell, I bet they act as each other's wingman. I will be mortified if everyone he works with knows. I do the occasional pop-in when I make cookies or invent a new desert recipe that I want to try on people. Baking is a silly little hobby I have, and I fantasize about creating a cookbook someday or starting my own little bakeshop. In fact, last year for Christmas I begged for a

Kitchen Aid industrial mixer and all I got was the most hideous purse from the retail store I work at during the holidays. I wonder what he got *her*.

"This sucks!" I snapped as I put his phone on the table by my side of the bed.

"I know, Shelly. I don't know how I feel." "So do you even love me?"

"Yes."

"Do you love her?"

"I don't know."

"Why is she still texting you? You are busted and she knows that. Does she actually think it's OK for the two of you to still be in contact with each other?"

"I don't know."

"Well it is *not* OK."

"I know."

"And I felt like a real ass being the one to try to make you stop. I am not your mother."

"I know that, Shelly. Come on. Let's go to sleep."

After brushing his teeth, Jim crawled onto my side of the bed, stuck the extra pillow in between our knees and spooned me for a long time as I cried into my pillow. No more words were spoken that night. Just tears and tears and tears.

I had horrible dreams for part of the night. One was about Jim and this woman coming in my line at the retail store while I took my shift at the register. I had to wait on the two of them. Another dream was harder to remember, but I was driving and the road kept swerving back and forth and I couldn't seem to slow down. The road was actually one that I travel on often to get to work and to take Theo to his trombone lesson. This road suddenly disappeared and I was flying for a moment before I awoke, startled. Jim was still in bed with me, but over on his side, no longer spooning me.

I did not sleep much after the second dream. I listened to Jim and the noises he made. He must have had a bad dream, too, as he talked a little and turned his head saying, "no, no." I turned toward him but not quite enough to spoon him. I was just close enough to smell him. I have always marveled at how odd it was that I do our laundry together, yet his clothes always smell so delightful. I sniff the clothes on me and smell nothing. On him they smell like a warm summer morning. Does he smell so divine simply because he is mine? At this point I don't even know if he is mine or hers. I sure wish the pastor had called back. I am trying to do what the cheating website said to do by giving him space, but I am an epic failure at that.

I prayed. I prayed for clarity, for hope, and for the peace that passes all understanding. At least for tonight, God's answer was a resounding "no." No peace and no understanding. I fell back asleep for a couple of hours before the alarm jolted me back into another crappy day as the wife of a cheating bastard.

Galatians 5:5
But by faith we eagerly await through the Spirit
of righteousness for which we hope.

CHAPTER SIX

408

*"It's hard to think about what you've wanted.
It's hard to think about what you've lost."*

Stop Draggin' My Heart Around
—*Tom Petty*

I stood at the kitchen counter staring at the phone I had been given the previous night. I clicked the phone on and scrolled through the menu. I discovered that my non-technologically minded nincompoop only knew how to delete the messages that *she* sent to *him*. He had never bothered to delete the messages that *he* sent to *her!* I saw what any woman would dread. The screen read "408 text messages." This meant that there were at least 816 texts back and forth in a four- or five-month period. I almost fainted. The blood in my body rushed down into the pit of my being, so I went over to sit on the living room couch.

Day seven of not eating anything sure didn't help the dizzy feeling as I stumbled to the couch. The weight of the phone itself was too much. Still, I just had to know what each and every one of those texts said. So with my calendar and pen, I began to read each and every one, writing down what day and time each text was sent.

I was trying to delete as I read, but I accidentally re-sent one. Crap! I tried to hit delete before it really sent, but it was too late. The quick reply from her was: *u r not supposed to contact me anymore ur wife texted me last night.*

I responded with: it's the wife. *just accidentally hit send instead of delete. just reading the 408 texts.*

Thus began the onslaught of texts back and forth with *"it."* Here are the highlights:

y would u do that? i guess i would 2 if this happened to me, she replied.

how long did this go on?
i think u and jim should talk about this
no, i want to know from you
about 4 months or so. we met in sept.
did u know he was married?"
yes, but we had an instant connection

Ugh! I think I just threw up in my mouth!

i need to know for my own safety if you guys did it, I continued.

i really think this is between u and jim. please let me walk away

so i guess by you not answering, that you two did do it? i need to know for my own safety if i should go to a doctor and get checked out

we only did it once, and i am really clean

Those words stung like a hot poker searing through my soul. I paused to absorb this. While waiting for breath to come back into my lungs, she continued.

being married 4 that long with 4 kids and bills, i can only imagine that those things can get in the way of romance. i was dealing with my own shit and we were having fun. he made me laugh and i stroked his ego a bit but we both knew it was wrong. please let me walk away. i hope in some strange way i have helped.

I was absolutely dumbfounded that she wrote this. She thought perhaps she had helped me? How? What fun to feel utterly used and defeated. What joy to be so humiliated. Such thrills to be faking eating around my kids and friends, and what a delight to question every little glance that Jim gives me. What an honor it is to follow him around all the time when he is at home so I know that he is not trying to make secret plans with her. Ya bitch. Big help. Still, the Christian side of me texted back, *ya, maybe you have.*

u have a great guy. take care of that fun loving, artsy man. try to enjoy life and live in the moment. namaste, she finished.

namaste, I replied.

Ugh! I can't believe I just texted her back basically saying that the divine in me recognizes the divine in her!

Sounds like this woman is into yoga, but if she really embraced the philosophy of a true yogi, she would know that with it comes spiritual codes and rituals, none of which involve hurting another being by screwing with another woman's husband!

This was about to be a long morning. Before continuing, I threw my calendar, pen and cell phone into my bag. Thinking that the coffee shop might be a more private place to go, I grabbed the car keys and left the house before Jim, Grace or Theo woke up to bother me.

Settling into the coffee shop couch with some hot tea to sip on, I read his texts to her.

stop smoking
please try

Gross. He was messing with a smoker? Drugs and smoking were always a deal-breaker for us. When Jim and I first dated, he would not even let me talk about my past when it came to recreational drugs and questionable friends. We always prided ourselves on being these amazing runners and we scoffed at people who did not share our love for fitness and health. We used to go to bars before no smoking laws, and bitch when we came home that we had to take a second shower that evening just to get the putrid smell of nicotine off of our clothes and hair. Does he like licking a dirty ashtray when he kisses her?

The next text read:
butter on u
stick form
how long will u b on me?

God, I don't even want to know about stick butter and their bodies on top of each other.

thanks for lunch
i want 2 play 2

So it wasn't just meeting at a sleazy bar and dancing. They had lunch.

i liked ur hot bod on me

Sent on a Monday, so I guess he was out with her on the weekend while I was working.

miss u. can't call. hope you like the book

This was one he forgot to delete from her, so I guess I have a book to look for after this. It was sent on his lunch hour. Oh, the times I wished he had been calling *me* on his lunch hour.

i will call u 2night
miss you xoxoxox

Holy crap! Those little letters hurt so much. Every Valentine's card, anniversary card and birth card ever given to me had those sweet little letters on them. Those were just for us.

i hope you are having a good day
i am happy you called

Yikes. I know of a lot of people who only text, because you can appear to be personal without seeing or hearing the person. But the two of them *talked* on *his* cell phone that *I* begged him to get! Talking is real. Talking is personal. Talking is what you do when you are in a relationship. Shit. This is brutal.

Again the tears, followed by rage, followed by utter and complete exhaustion. I called work from my cell phone and took a sick day. No way could I fake it today.

c u then
i need a sign to let me know u r here
ur luv is so good hannah

Ah Ha! I now have a name. But did he say "love"?

what is hannah up 2 today?
miss u. need u

Did I just throw up bile in my mouth? Yep, sure tastes like it. Yummy bile.

need 2 spoon u soon
i will have a happy face if I c u 2 day

Spooning? Hey, that too is *our* thing.

i will be ur stripper
i bring my own pole
c u 2 night

Again, bile taste in my mouth, as the date of this text was *my freaking birthday!*

luv u. hope it's ok 2 feel it

do not use me. luv me
i wish I could be in ur arms
good morning. how r u?
i will get out somehow 2 day
ur tears fell into my heart. luv u
oh silly hannah, u know what 2 do with me
missing u a fuckin' lot. did tyler have fun?
Oh my God, was that a text about them doing something together with her kid? I guess four kids of his own isn't enough to spend time with.
i c u every day in the ipod songs. Thanks a lot
iPod? Jim doesn't own an iPod. Being the ever-frugal man, he has a knock-off brand that he uses when he runs. Well, now I have something else to search for besides a book. So, this *thing* (I can't even bring myself to say *woman*) showers *my* man with presents?
do u know ur plans 4 2 night?
c u @ sam's fitness?
u have a hot bod. when we come together we r superbod
Yahoo! I also get to see where the hell Sam's Fitness is. Oh the snooping and research I get to do in my spare time.
i enjoyed being w/u and tyler
make sure you move the broken chair so tyler doesn't get hurt
Crap! He was definitely in *her house!* I only hope to God she was never at our home when our own children were out. I don't think I could live with the knowledge of her being in *my* space.
sorry i keep calling u. i am bored out of my mind
should be able to get out to go on a hike
silly hannah. any place in ur heart makes me happy
c u sunday

Of course he saw her Sunday. That is a given I would be working that stupid holiday job. Note to self: *Quit now!*

This next one was sent on New Year's Day, and it cut me to the core. It read: *the party was no fun. same old-same old*

thanks. u r an amazing woman. i know u care about me and that will bring me up

So, the party was no fun? I thought it was. Every year for the last eight or nine years, we go to a good friend's house for New Year's Eve. We see good friends from our neighborhood and from the school our children attend. The catered food is amazing. They rent one of those heated tents to accommodate more guests than their home will fit, and a small band plays. It is the one party each year where children are forbidden. Just grown-up time. I love getting dressed up and having the champagne toast at midnight. I love the whole idea of another fresh start and another year with the man I have loved since I was 22. Obviously my Jimmy was making a fresh start with someone else, while playing husband to me and daddy to our kids.

thanks for the sex text. my concentration is shot. hope u stay in 2 night

still thinking about that one. u get off by now

maybe i could babysit tyler and u could come home horny

Reading this was too much. The tears began to fall and fall and then flood into the coffee shop napkins I grabbed from the counter.

So personal. So intimate. So sexual. So wrong. My man and *another* woman sharing sexy thoughts, feelings, and intimate conversation. I dry heaved into the napkin and got some concerned looks from another customer. Nothing came up but a metallic taste. Tea. I need to drink the tea. There are no more tears and no more liquids anywhere in my body to rid myself of. I am dry. I am parched. I am spent. Yet I read on.

> *i could run by your house around 4:45*

She must live close to his work since he gets off at 4:30.

> *c u friday. stop smoking. i mean it*

Oh how sweet to try to save her from her wretched habit. What a saint I married.

> *regretting not seeing u 2 day*
>
> *going 4 a run. c u @ 3*
>
> *u r my reality. caring about u and being with u is real*
>
> *i sleep with u in me*
>
> *when i look into your amazing green eyes i c a beautiful, young girl so full of life*
>
> *no, i am happy that i met u*
>
> *u r telling me 2 stop loving u. that won't be easy*
>
> *i will stop if it is what u want. i understand.*
>
> *u r taking a big step in the direction u want to go in ur life. maybe in time we could b friends*
>
> *hard to make it through the day without hearing from u*
>
> *i am no longer the master of my emotions*
>
> *do u want 2 c me?*
>
> *u r right. we need to talk face 2 face*
>
> *it's hard to stop my thoughts and feeling 4 u. please don't b 2 mad that I called u.*
>
> *2day would be good. sorry no tyler*
>
> *can u talk by phone?*
>
> *i feel very alone. r u out there?*
>
> *we both know I need to c u tonight. we need 2 say goodbye*

This slew of texts ironically came a few days before I caught him throwing the phone under the sheets. Were they trying to break up and they just couldn't? Did he know on some level that he may get caught soon? I can only hope that they were figuring out by this point that they were getting way too serious and things would be getting way too complicated. Could the texts get any more personal and intimate? I was almost done. I had to persevere.

my heart soars with the fucking birds when I hear from u

Yep. They were getting worse. Jim had never talked to me in this manner, even when we were in our 20s and dating. I thought we were head over heels, but apparently that was just me. I know there was no such thing as texting back then, but still, I have no love letters of this nature to reflect upon. In fact, when we had to write something endearing about each other in our wedding album, it took several months of me prompting him to just write a couple of lines. XOXO was just about the only romantic thing I got from him in writing, and now I feel as if those letters don't even count!

silly hannah, the birds will understand
c u @ 12:00
i am inside
fuck ya, I had a great time
miss u
where r u?
2 night ok?
ya, u and me alone is better
good morning beautiful
oh ya, u looked great in my shirt

Now wait a minute. The date of this text was when I was in town. None of our children had games, concerts or meets that day. When did they find time to hang out long enough for her to be wearing his shirt? Was this the time they had sex? I winced at the thought.

The next texts were dated after the night I took his phone from him. I had already erased the nasty text about her wanting to be in his pants.

i need to call u. hope u r ok
text when u can. hell of a day
silly hannah, love stinks. I'm ok
87.5 listen now
u missed r song bitch

He was referring to a radio station. College radio. I used to listen to 87.5 in the '90s when I was a huge Morrissey fan. I heard my first B52's song, my first Morrissey song and my first Psychedelic Furs song on college radio. So *my* Jimmy and that *thing* have a song. In our 25 years of marriage, there have been plenty of songs that made me think of Jim and I am sure a few that he may associate with me, but we never officially had *a* song. Again, I am broken, confused, depressed, and exhausted. I know it seems so junior high school, but I am completely jealous of this woman and the power she has over my husband to turn him into a lovesick boy again. I am not sure I can get up from the coffee shop couch when I am startled by my cell phone ringing.

It was Grace. "Mommy, where are you? Did you forget that I have swimming today? Daddy went to the hardware store to get something and there is no car for Theo to take me."

Quoting the lyrics of Soul to Soul "Back to life. Back to reality," I respond. "I'll be there soon. Pack your swim bag and I will see you in 10 minutes."

Just a few more to read. Grace can be late to swimming.

good morning hannah
ok 2 work out again friday?
no outcome. it seems 2 b up 2 me

don't know y i am up
missing u like crazy. xoxox
let me c u. trouble or not
will try 2 get out 2 c u 2day

Sounds like they were trying to break up, as I had guessed, but they were still playing with fire.

sorry my heart wont stop
no matter where we r, r hearts r 2gether
goodnight
i miss tyler
fri or sat best night 2 run into u?
i have no plan
good song on
ya, give me a shout out
any song from u is 4 me
c u @ sam's fitness
great song, thanks
silly hannah, I do miss u

That was the last text I saw before Jim surrendered the phone to me. I was blown away by how many of those texts had dates and times after I caught him throwing the phone under the sheets. As I drove home to pick up Grace, all I could do was wonder if it was my fault. I wondered what I did to push Jim out and make him even think of looking for another woman. That horrible phrase kept rolling through my head. *We had an instant connection... connection... connection... connection.*

After taking Gracie to swimming, I got a call from the associate pastor saying that he had received my message and that the head pastor was out of town. Was there anything he could do? I graciously declined and said that I would wait until Pastor Gary was back to schedule a meeting. After seeing the massive amount of personal texts, I was questioning what Pastor Gary could even do to resurrect this marriage.

Psalms 119:116
Sustain me according to your promise, and I will live; do not let my hopes be dashed.

CHAPTER SEVEN

The Poignant Sermon

*"There is hope for the helpless, rest for the weary
and love for the broken hearts.
There is grace and forgiveness, mercy and healing.
He'll meet you wherever you are.
Cry out to Jesus. Cry out to Jesus."*

Cry Out to Jesus
—Third Day

We let the kids sleep in and miss church. Maybe Jim knew there would be too many tears in church today. I am one of those sappy people who cries at a Hallmark commercial, and I have never made it through one Christmas service without blubbering like a sap when they play the old hymns mixed in with the contemporary service we go to. Today, however, the tears would be more for the love lost, the lies, the sadness and the confusion we were both feeling.

So what was the sermon on today? Forgiveness! How does God do that? He always seems to have a poignant sermon aimed right at whatever I am dealing with. The associate pastor was amazing. He started with speaking about the blame that went on in Genesis. When God went looking for Adam and Eve, they were hiding because they were naked. God asked if Adam had eaten from the forbidden tree. Adam blamed Eve, then Eve blamed the serpent. No one said "Gee, God, yes I did eat from the forbidden tree and I am really, really sorry." What would our lives be like now if Adam had just apologized?

Later the pastor spoke about various types of forgiveness. There is the forgiveness we ask for, the forgiveness we offer to others and the forgiveness that we receive. There is also withholding forgiveness, but he was going to save that one for another day. I was stuck on his words about forgiving others. I know I really needed to forgive Jim, but I had not even thought that I also needed to forgive Hannah. In her texts to me she said she was "dealing with her own shit" which could have meant anything. Why didn't she marry Tyler's father? What was he like? Does he take care of them financially? Why is she still out at bars looking for love in all the wrong places? What's it like to be a single mom? I bet she has a hard time making all of the decisions for her and Tyler. I bet she gets tired. I bet if I were in that situation, I'd be looking for an older, responsible man to take care of me and my baby.

I decided at that moment to forgive her as well. I prayed through the silent tears that had been welling up all morning. Jim tried hard to look straight ahead, but he grabbed my hand and gave it the tender and warm squeeze that I needed. Interestingly, as I was praying for her, I felt a sense of peace, but I knew that I would not be able to just shrug everything off now and be OK. The saying "forgive and forget" is a bit of a stretch. Even the pastor said that in some situations we may be able to forgive, but we will never, ever forget. So in essence, he was letting me know that it's OK to feel whatever I was feeling.

The pastor also quoted something from the Book of Matthew, when Matthew was trying to find out from Jesus when it was OK to be really angry. Jesus responded by asking Matthew if he really wanted all of that anger to fester and stew. Crap. Speaking to me again. This was going to be harder than I thought, as I was still feeling anger, along with the feeling of inadequacy that comes with knowing you were not enough to please and satisfy your own husband.

In the car, I told Jim that I forgave her. I'm not sure what he was feeling, as he was rather silent the whole way home. I guess he was just relieved that church was over and that he could go on with his Sunday with the kids as I went to my retail job—and gave them my two weeks' notice.

My manager at work seemed sad to see me go. When I told the lady who does the scheduling, I hinted as to why I was leaving. I am not sure if she picked up my undertones, but I think she did.

"You have to do what you have to do," she said. "You know you can always come back," she added as I left for my shift.

Before starting the car to go home, I called my sister Jennifer from my cell phone. I told her about the latest development: seeing the texts that Jim had sent to *it*.

"Oh, Shelly, I am so sorry. Sounds like it was more involved than you thought. What can I do? More important, what are *you* going to do?"

"Well, I still love the son of a bitch."

"I know. You always see the good in people, and you never give up." she said.

"Thanks. He says we can see the pastor. That's a good sign that he wants to work things out."

"Is it that old geezer who preached when I was up to visit last time?"

"Oh no. This guy is older than we are, but so lively and accurate in how he approaches the Bible. He reminds me of the pastor I liked so much when we went to church camp. Do you remember the summer mom sent us to a one-week church camp?"

"How could I forget?" Jennifer exclaimed. "I think I had my first make-out session with some guy from the boy cabins when we were supposed to be singing 'Kumbaya.' I think his name was Simon or Stan or something."

I can always count on my horny sister to remember something about boys or sex. She has always been the wild card in our family. When we were little, her favorite bedtime story was about a little dog that had no owner. He was just an independent little mutt who belonged to himself. My favorite book was one about being a little mommy. I even remember the first few pages. I think it started with "This is my house and I am the mommy. My children are Annabelle, Betsy and Bonnie. They are good little children and do just as I say... *something, something, something* and they go out to play." So funny how we grew up so differently. Still, I knew she would be sympathetic and I really can't fathom any of my friends knowing about this yet. It is just so embarrassing. I don't want my friends to look at me any differently or feel sorry for me. I do enough of that on my own.

Jennifer seemed genuinely thrilled as I spoke about the forgiveness sermon and how I had actually prayed for Hannah as I silently forgave her for what she did to Jim's heart.

"Oh, you are so brave. When I was married, all I could think of was revenge."

"But you were happy for a while, weren't you?"

"I thought I was, but I think we really just didn't know each other well enough from the beginning. I mean, geez... we got married after only three months. I didn't even know his favorite color, let alone that he was a womanizing creep!"

My sister has been divorced for over 13 years. I am shocked at how the anger still sounds so fresh. I sure hope this isn't me years down the road.

"Your situation is different," she continued.

"How so?" I asked.

"You and Jimmy dated for such a long time before you got married, and you waited a couple of years before having kids. I think you really got to know him before all the complications of a family. I swear this sounds like a mid-life crisis more than a habitual thing, like with my ex," she reassured me.

Jennifer had another call, but promised that I could call her anytime I needed a good cry and a great listener. Mid-life crisis. Yes, let's hope that it is just a stupid mid-life crisis and not some new lifestyle he is committed to.

Acts 14:22
Strengthening the disciples and encouraging them
to remain true to the faith, "We must go through many
hardships to enter the kingdom of God," they said.

CHAPTER EIGHT
My Assignment

"So you thought you had to keep this up.
All the work that you do, so we think that you're good.
And you can't believe it's not enough."

Healing Begins
—Tenth Avenue North

I told Jim that I had given my two weeks' notice. I felt a sort of sadness, as I had been there throughout the holiday season for the last five years and had made some great friends. Still, I had to wonder if leaving Jim alone all of those Friday and Saturday nights to go drinking with his guy friend Marcus was such a great idea. I even entertained the idea that I was the one responsible for his having had the affair in the first place. Maybe I was too tired and crabby to really be there for him. Here I thought I was helping the family by bringing in extra income when really all we needed was to be together more. Rolling those thoughts of blame through my head made the night drag on and on. I feigned wanting to finish a book, so I retired to the bedroom with said book. Once there I took my favorite worn pillow and let Niagara fall all over again.

The pastor came back in town on Monday and when he heard my story, he agreed to see us the very next day. He wasn't a marriage counselor per se, but he did have the smarts to first talk to us together, then send me down the hall to talk to Jim alone. I had my Bible with me and was pretending to read it. I was really just being still and quiet, wondering what the hell he was telling the pastor that he and that woman did. I was at least three rooms away, and there was no way to eavesdrop.

Next he sent Jim down the hall to talk to me alone. I cried miserably. I blubbered about none of this making any sense when all I have ever done is just loved and loved and loved Jim for all of these years. I knew some part of it had to do with him not being very spiritual. His parents were rather dysfunctional, and there was some abuse I had heard about in bits and pieces at family gatherings. I ventured a thought that perhaps only a person who felt unloved in some way would try to validate that by seeing who else might love him. The pastor just listened with no judgment and no comment.

When he brought us back in the same room together, the pastor asked us a simple question that blew me away: "What do you guys want to do?"

What?! As a pastor and man of God (God hates divorce), shouldn't he be doing *everything* in his power to help us get through this?

Jim spoke first with "Fix it." What a relief! If I voted to fix it first, and Jim voted to do the same out of guilt, then where would we be? I doubt that we could really live in a happy and successful marriage if he was just being coerced into being with me. He seemed sincere in his statement.

"That's my vote too," I squeaked.

It came out that Jim views me as a judgmental person who doesn't like to dance or drink. Judgmental? I had stopped telling Jim years ago about my *real* goals and dreams for fear of *his* judgment towards *me*. I don't enjoy dancing in front of him because one time he actually told me how to move my hips! I thought dancing was supposed to be your own body interpreting the music. I was so embarrassed that he was telling me how to dance, that I never wanted to dance again after that night. I never told him about this. In hindsight, maybe I should have.

I never told Jim what I really wanted in bed from him for fear of having him judge me there, too. I have a hobby of baking, and wanted to explore that as a little cottage industry business, but I am always afraid to ask Jim for the seed money to get it off the ground. I have a desire to go from 5Ks and 10Ks back into full marathons, but I am nervous that he will judge my slowness after popping out all of those kids and then taking several years in the too-busy-to-take-care-of-me-because-I-have-kids mode. How is it that he sees in me the very things I see in him? It made me wonder if we had been judging each other falsely all of these years. Why were so many of our conversations guarded? I wish it were easier to express my true self in front of him.

I wondered if Jim was holding back from me too, and not telling me *his* real hopes, dreams, aspirations, fantasies and so on, for fear of *my* judgment. If so, then how many years did we waste, holding back on a true friendship? We seem to have put up some fairly tall walls around our true emotions.

I tried as hard as I could to tell both of these men that I simply could not understand why Jim was giving Hannah the very things that I had been begging him for, for years. For a long time I have been begging Jim for dates. OK, so maybe they were not drinking and dancing dates, but I love going to rock concerts, having dinner, seeing movies, hanging out with other couples and so on. For years I have wanted to start running with Jim again, like we used to do with the kids in the baby strollers. He is much faster than I am, so he always has an excuse not to run with me, and yet according to the texts, he was working out at a fitness club with a 40-something smoker? How fast could *she* possibly run?

I had been asking him for more quality time, like meeting for lunch at his work, but he always said if he skipped lunch he could get home earlier, so I never bothered him at work. The texts read *thanks 4 lunch*, so once again, it seems like Hannah got all of the things I felt I deserved.

At the end of our meeting, the pastor gave me an assignment. It was to just lighten up and go have a drink and dance with my husband. Profound huh? Oh boy. I wasn't sure if he gave Jim an assignment also when they spoke alone, and I did not have the courage to ask. Before we left, Pastor Gary pulled me aside and said, "Just give him some space. He needs to figure this out." Space? When Jim and Pastor G. were alone did he say something about me hanging on him all the time or following him from room to room? I guess I have done that a bit lately, because I am so freaking insecure. I want to snoop and make sure he isn't calling her.

The rest of the week was spent flipping out over my assignment to start drinking and dancing. I had not danced in front of him in over 14 years. When I passed in front of a mirror, I would strut a bit and I couldn't even do *that* without laughing at myself. When did I get so ill at ease in my own body? I used to dance every weekend with my girlfriends when I was in my 20s. Has raising kids made me feel so old that I can't cut loose anymore?

Much to Jim's relief, on day 11 of my great depression, I decided to eat again. A 12-pound weight loss was noticeable enough and hard to explain in February, when everyone is still fat from Thanksgiving, Christmas and New Year's. Jim had been trying to get me to eat for days, and I kept giving him the same reason: I just couldn't fathom eating. My entire life was so out of control, that eating (or in this case *not* eating) was the only thing that I *could* control. It felt nice to be able to control at least this *one* thing. He understood my reasoning to a point. Still, he seemed genuinely concerned for my health. Being a genetic anomaly, Jim has only gained or lost about three pounds since I have known him. He cannot understand the fluctuations of a woman's body, especially under stress. I am not sure if he will ever understand that eating is an emotional thing as well as a physical need.

I really wanted Jim to be with me when I ate my first solid food again, so we went to my favorite Thai place. I had about a quarter of the tofu and coconut soup, and part of a rice and banana desert. I don't think he was impressed, but I was proud that I choked that much down.

Saturday night came. He wore a sexy pair of jeans I purchased for him at Christmas when I was oblivious to the fact that he was most likely wearing them with *her.* His gray, long-sleeved shirt was tight at the forearms, and they made him look like he lifts more weights than he actually does. Again, a genetic anomaly. I had no idea what to wear, so I asked him.

"Wear what you want. I'm just wearing jeans and a shirt."

"Yeah, I see that, but what would you like to see me in?" I pressed.

"I don't care. Whatever you want."

OK, this was not helpful. Jim has always told me that guys are so visual. Any time I had ever seen porn make its way into our house, I would ask what the hell he needed that for, and he would just shrug and say, "Guys are visual. It's no big deal." So here I am trying to appeal to his "visual" nature, and he couldn't give a rat's ass. Great. So on went my jeans, black boots, a T-shirt with flowers on it and a thin jacket that hung long in the front. I applied minimal make up, and off we went on our date.

Having not had a drink in at least five years (other than a champagne toast on New Year's Eve and an occasional sip of his beer while we watched TV), and knowing that I had to dance, I drank. I drank some more. Four drinks later I was dancing. I tried as hard as I could to look at the other people dancing and not at my own husband. I was too terrified that Jim would be stifling his laughter at the buffoon in front of him, otherwise known as his wife.

We stayed for most of the second set of the band before deciding to leave. I looked around one last time, thankful that there was no one in this dive I knew. In the car, things started to spin, and I knew I had made a very big mistake. Losing 12 pounds and drinking for the first time in years is not a combination I recommend. Shockingly I made it inside the house before I did all of the gut heaving in the bathroom, but Jim was less than sympathetic as he left me alone to clean up. I sat on the cold bathroom floor, stunned that he didn't even hold my hair back while I puked my guts into the downstairs toilet. It was really fun crawling upstairs to the other bathroom to barf some more before pouring myself next to an already asleep lump. What a waste of a buzz.

I woke the next morning wondering what part of drinking and dancing was fun. Was it the sticky dance floor, the disgusting bathrooms, the useless alcohol, skanky women, desperate men or loud music? Still, I had made it through the night and was ready to do whatever it took to keep our marriage together. If he needed to drink, dance and feel young again, I was ready. Bring it on.

I was thankful that Jim never mentioned how ridiculous I must have looked dancing, but I was disappointed that he didn't ask me how I was doing after the lovely vomit session I had all alone. If it was Hannah puking her guts out, I imagine he would have held *her* hair back and offered up his T-shirt to change into.

Sickening thoughts like that started my day, yet contradictory feelings were washing over me like a sunburn on a red head. In one moment I was feeling the extreme pain of the reality of Jim's infidelity, while in the next moment, I was feeling aroused, like I still had an alcohol buzz. I figured the horny feeling must be some deep-seeded need to show myself that *I* am the one who can make Jim happy. Maybe I just wanted him more because someone else wanted him, too. Will this horrendous event make me appreciate him more now that I know he can turn on other women?

"So, if we take quick showers, can we spend a little time in bed this morning?" I asked.

"Aren't you hung over?" he responded.

"No, I puked out all of the alcohol and a few organs, Jimmy!"

"I'll shower first," he said.

When he returned smelling like the peppermint aromatherapy soap I love so much, I jumped up to get my shower, too. Head rush. Down I went, back onto the bed.

"Are you sure this is a good idea?"

"I'm fine. I just get head rushes a lot since my weight loss. I'll be right back."

Our morning was spent finishing up what we should have done last night if I had not gotten sick. We rushed a little, as it is never as much fun when the kids are already up and starting their day. Thin walls make up the Rohner house!

Romans 13:8
Let no debt remain outstanding, except the
continuing debt to love one another,
for he who loves his fellowman
had fulfilled the law.

CHAPTER NINE

Research

"My whole world is the pain inside me. The best I can do is just get through the day. When life before is only a memory, I'll wonder why God lets me walk through this place."

Beauty From Pain
—*Superchick*

Ah, a new week. I was only scheduled for three days at my regular day job, so I anxiously awaited Jim's departure for work so I could dig around to find the book and the iPod Hannah had given him. I found the book first. It was a fairly expensive hardback about bike riding and bike racing. Jim and I have had various running injuries over the years and have occasionally used the bike to recover from years of competitive running. He must have shared that information with her.

The iPod was harder to find, as it was the tiny shuffle version. I found it in the inside pocket of Jimmy's ski jacket. I had some time to kill, so I turned it on and got on the treadmill. Holy cow! That woman had premeditated each and every song. The first song was about cheating, called "Lips of an Angel" by Hinder. I cried all the way through the lyrics. The entire song is a saga of a couple that still dreams about each other and has strong feelings, while he is currently living with someone else. Lyrics reveal how the current girl is in the next room without a clue, but what a fight will ensue if she figures out who called.

Next, Ben Harper was harping about "always have to steal my kisses from you," while Adele was busting out "I can't help feeling we could have had it all" from her Rolling in the Deep song.

Rihanna was singing about love found in a hopeless place, The Beatles were singing "All You Need is Love." Amy Winehouse was singing "Our day will come, and we'll have everything. We'll share the joy falling in love can bring." Seal was singing "Kiss By a Rose" (a soulful recount of being in a dark place before he meets his love) filled with gorgeous lyrics like, "you became the light on the dark side of me. Love remained a drug that's the high and not the pill."

Some of these sweet, love songs were mingled in with disgusting, sex songs, like Nine Inch Nails' "I Wanna Fuck You Like an Animal" and Gwen Stefani singing "...but I still love to wash in your old bathwater, love to think you couldn't love another." And how about Kings of Leon cranking out "Sex on Fire"? The sickest, most vile and offensive song was "Crazy Bitch" by Buck Cherry. Here the "F" bomb is dropped numerous times as the singer describes kinky and violent sex complete with scratches up the back and the need to video tape the carnal episode. What would possess anyone to enjoy listening to a song about sadomasochism? What was she trying to accomplish by putting that on the iPod? Is that how she wants to be treated after she puts her little baby to bed?

I remember as a teen, listening to some raunchy stuff, but it paled by comparison to this depravity. My father used to argue with me about the lyrics and I always used the same excuse. I would tell him that I just liked the beat and didn't listen to the lyrics. But I did. I listened and I allowed media to help shape my thoughts and sometimes my actions. Perhaps I read too much into a simple song, but perhaps not.

Next on the playlist was the Black Keys singing "Lonely Boy," where they sang: "I've got a love that keeps me waiting," and Katy Perry was singing, "You're so hypnotizing. You could be the devil. You could be an angel. Your touch is magnetizing."

The tamer songs included Prince's "I Would Die 4 U," and Average White Band's "Pick up the Pieces." I am sure that she didn't know that Jim and I used to go to Average White Band concerts back in the '80s. She had no way of knowing that I had a mild obsession with the movie Purple Rain. She didn't know that I crank my treadmill to Kings of Leon. She wasn't the one who bought Jim a Seal record for his birthday. Now, I will never be able to hear those songs and have the same memories. She took memories from me. She changed them. She ruined them. The damned nerve of her!

There were about 50 songs in all, and I was sick all over again. I went to my computer to restore the iPod to its original settings and *that's* how I found out her full name. I plugged it in off of my iPod cord and it read "Hannah E. McCabe's iPod."

The first place I went to snoop was a website called Spokeo. It gives the name, part of the address, part of the phone number, age, religion, and part of the family tree. If you want to pay, you can get more information. I knew I only needed to know the basics. I wanted to know how accurate the information was, so I searched under my name also. Wow. It even had my zodiac sign and everything was accurate except my religion. Heck, after the day I was having, I was about to lose my religion! I found other websites like freephonetracer.com, peoplesmart.com—and even the Internet yellow pages had a service to look up names from phone numbers—but they all charged to actually give you the name. Only the state, general location and the fact that it was a cell phone was given for free.

Next I discovered that you can look at someone's personal profile on Facebook without "friending" them. Oh my goodness. There she was on my laptop. Big green eyes, as Jim's text said, and curly, red shoulder-length hair. It wasn't fiery red like orphan Annie, but more like the copper of an old penny. Pretty, yet aged, perhaps from years of smoking, or maybe from the stresses of being a single mom. There were enough photos on her public profile that I even got to see her dear little child. The scary thing was, as I hovered my mouse over "mutual friends," I saw that we had two in common. Not close friends, mind you, but I realized that this woman was terrifyingly real and lived in the same 15-mile radius as my own family.

The phone rang as I was closing out the Facebook page. It was my neighbor Noreen and she talked my ear off about wanting to get back into shape. The neighborhood ladies know I am a runner, and she wanted to know if I was interested in helping her get back into her skinny jeans. I was struck with an idea.

"Well, Noreen, I was thinking we could take a trip up to Sam's Fitness and see if they have any membership specials," I said.

"I thought you and Jimmy hated those places and thought they were a waste of money."

"Most of the time I agree, but I am getting sick of the treadmill and maybe it's time for me to learn to swim or take a Zumba class or something," I lied.

"Want me to drive?" she asked.

"Sure."

There it was: an opportunity to visit the place where my husband worked out with the smoker. Off we went. I made small talk about how Rob and Rich were doing well their first year away from each other, and she made small talk about her daughter starting cheerleading at the gymnastics center in town. I wanted to tell her more personal stuff, but something told me to just shut up and let her ramble.

We pulled into a large parking lot filled primarily with SUVs and vans. It must be a soccer mom's haven or a yuppie place to work out. Inside we were greeted by two ladies in Sam's Fitness polo shirts with clipboards. They were more than happy to have us fill out a two-page questionnaire. I lied about my last name and phone number as I nervously looked around for the red-headed home-wrecker. We received the full tour of the indoor pool, outdoor pool, sauna, locker rooms, basketball courts, rock climbing wall, spinning rooms and yoga rooms. On the next floor there was a huge room with over a dozen elliptical machines, at least 20 treadmills, weight machines and some free weights. We peeked in on a Pilates class and saw where the day care was for working parents. There was a juice bar/cafe that seemed quite trendy with its décor and menu of raw juices, kale chips, seaweed and the like. This place even had a tanning salon and a place for manicures and pedicures.

Before we had a chance to breathe we were shuffled into a small room that reminded me of being in a car dealership.

Our lovely, fit and fake-tanned tour guides turned us over to a gentleman, also in a matching polo. I knew his job would be to try and bamboozle us into a lifelong membership for a "steal." I appeared interested for Noreen's sake, but knew that my soul purpose of visiting today was to see and feel the pain of knowing that my Jimmy had spent time in here sweating with Hannah. Let me say it again: sweating with Hannah. Ugh! She got to see my beautiful man in running shorts and tank top, glistening with sweat. Too real. This was perhaps too much information. I knew I would spend the rest of the day questioning why on earth I had to snoop.

Noreen and I took the salesman's business card and left. I could barely talk on the way home. Back in the confines of my own domain, I went to my computer and cleared out the songs that were on Hanna's iPod, only to replace them with my own tragic songs. I took some of my favorite depressing songs and made a CD for myself too. I have heard that alcoholics cannot fully recover until they hit rock bottom. Maybe I needed to hit a sort-of rock bottom also. The rationale of making this depressing CD was, the sooner I could hit rock bottom, the sooner I could start healing. The sooner I get this out of me, the sooner I can get back to concentrating on being the wife, mom and friend I was before all of this bullshit occurred.

1 Corinthians 16:13-14
Be on your guard; stand firm in the faith;
be men of courage; be strong.
Do everything in love.

CHAPTER TEN
Songs

"...how quick the sun can drop away. And now my bitter hands cradle broken glass of what was everything... all the love gone bad, turned my world to black."

Black
—Pearl Jam

I started my playlist with Melanie Fiona's "4 AM." This song ripped through me one day while flipping through radio stations shortly before the worst night of my life. I remembered the lyrics enough to then find the song and buy it. It would work well for the sole purpose of falling deeper into this pit of despair.

Melody describes how crazy she feels in a relationship where the man does not come home or answer the phone. She imagines what he must be doing and with whom. With pain and anguish in her voice, she waits in his bed. She, like me, had no idea how bruised a heart can get. The anger swells in her as the hours tick by and her calls go unanswered. She feels that she would make the perfect wife and just wants her mans time.

I think that must be universal. All we really want from the love of our lives is time together. Pure and simple, *time*.

I put "Precious" right after "4 AM." In this Depeche Mode fantasy I pretend that Jim would realize how badly he and *miss thing* wrecked me. And in my warped fantasy of hell, he would burst out in song and apologize with the haunting words of Martin Gore and the steamy, baritone voice of David Gahan singing, "Precious and fragile things need special handling. My God what have we done to you?"

He sings about how angels should not know suffering and perhaps God has a master plan. He sings about hoping that faith and trust can be restored.

Did Martin Gore read my diary? How can one song sum up how fragile a relationship can be? I want to be that angel who knows no suffering. I want Jim to be that singer who feels bad about what he has put me through as he asks for forgiveness. I want to be that person who keeps room in my heart for the two of us. Now, I know that Jim doesn't even sing in the shower, so I know he will never burst into song for me, but heck, it's my fantasy, right?

I also threw on there Morrissey with "I am Hated for Loving You," Luther Vandross' "A House is not a Home," Jessie J.'s "Big White Room," Puddle of Mudd's "Blurry," Pearl Jam's "Black," Morrissey's "You Should Have Been Nice to Me," Joni Mitchel's "Blue," Kings of Leon's "Cold Desert," Kanye West's "Heartless," Pillar's "Chasing Shadows at Midnight," Pat Benetar's "Love is a Battlefield," Elton John's "Love Song," and Morrissey's "Black Cloud." I earmarked more for a second disc, but this was great for starters.

I was home when Jim came through the door and ran to the land line. He dialed and I heard him say "Um, yes, it's Jimmy again. Could I have you play Adele and do a shout out to Gracie." Jim then proceeded to go to the living room radio and put it on college radio. How cute that he requested a song for his daughter. We started looking over the mail that came and I was deciding what I should make for dinner. Theo wanted tacos and Grace wanted pizza. Gracie is daddy's little princess, so I figured we would be eating pizza again.

The Adele song was played soon after I took a pizza from the freezer, and I got the brilliant idea to request a song for Jim. I went to the Internet to look up the radio station's phone number while Jim went upstairs. I called the station and got a woman on the other line.

"Yes, I'd like to request a song for Jimmy."

"Oh! Is this Hannah?" she asked.

Now remember, this is college radio and not that many people call in. I could totally see how a DJ could get to know the people who call in regularly. And I had *no* filter on that big mouth of mine. I took the portable phone and walked down to the basement where I hoped to be out of earshot of Grace and Theo.

"No! This is Jimmy's wife, and to my knowledge, Hannah and Jimmy were supposed to *stop* sending songs to each other!" I snapped.

I continued to give her an earful of anger. "Oh... well. I just didn't know because I have never heard her voice. She hasn't ever called in," the DJ responded.

Bull! I thought she did a glorious job of trying to backpedal and lie her way out of that one. Those texts made it all too clear that Jim and *it* were sending love songs to each other.

Crushed again, I went up to tell Jim what had just transpired but he was already out the door in his running clothes. I caught him by the mailbox and told him what happened. He just gave me a dumb look and said, "I'm gonna go for a run."

When he came home, he found me, pulled me into our room and threw his sweaty arms around me.

"I'm really sorry," he said.

"For what?"

"For running away like a coward."

He said he had not called songs in that much and had not done it recently for anyone but Gracie. I was not sure if I should have believed him, but in between listening to my sad songs, as well as having my early morning cry, I started listening to a lot more college radio, too—just in case there were any good requests.

"Mom, I'm out of books. Can I take your car to the library after dinner?" asked Theo.

"Actually, I could get a book or two, too." I answered.

Ah, the geek in the family. Our Theo used to swim and play soccer when he was younger, but over the last few years has gotten serious about his trombone and his avid reading. He sets these crazy goals for reading a certain number of books in a school quarter, and usually hits the mark with a book or two to spare. We really should buy that kid a Kindle.

At the library I browsed through books about relationships. Can you imagine that there are even books about cheating? I knew I could not put those on my library card in front of Theo, so I read what I could while he picked out his novels. As we were about to leave, I grabbed several relationship books and a few mysteries to place on top of the pile in case Theo was paying attention to my selections.

Back at home I saw Jim looking all over the house as if he had lost something. "What ya lookin' for?" I asked.

"Oh, just my MP3 player."

"I think I saw it in the man cave," I replied.

"Oh."

Funny he didn't say *iPod*. I'm sure it was because he didn't know that I knew he had a real, Apple iPod, and he didn't know that I now had possession of it. I felt a bit smug as I made a batch of cookies for the kids. Baking has always been a great distraction for me when I have too much on my mind. On this night, however, the smugness wore off as I felt convicted and compelled to tell Jim the truth.

When I brought a plate of cookies up to our bedroom, I told Jim that maybe our marriage was worse off than I thought.

"Why do you say that?" he asked.

"Well, I lied to you earlier today," I confessed.

"About what?"

"You asked if I had seen your MP3 player and I knew you meant this iPod," I said as I pulled from my pocket the little blue stick.

"Where did you get this?" he asked, quite shocked.

"In your ski jacket pocket. I listened to the songs and they were gross. I knew this must have been something *she* gave you." He went to take it from my hand and I pulled back.

"I took the songs off of there, Jimmy! Do you really want to listen to the songs that will remind you of *her?!*"

"There were some good songs on there. So it has nothing on it now?" he asked.

"Well, I put my own songs on there. I think it's my iPod now."

He had nothing to say after that. Leaving the cookies on the night table, he looked sheepish as he climbed into bed. He made a feeble attempt to redeem himself by snuggling really close and kissing the back of my neck, but I curled up into fetal position and cried myself to sleep, silently praying to erase all doubt that we can still save this marriage.

James 1:6
But when he asks, he must believe and not doubt,
because he who doubts is like
a wave of the sea, blown
and tossed by the wind.

CHAPTER ELEVEN

The Funeral

"Here is the house where it all happens.
Those tender moments under this roof.
Body and soul come together as we come closer together."

Here is the House
—Depeche Mode

The phone rang as I was heading out the door to work. It was my mother-in-law calling to say that Jimmy's second cousin had died suddenly of a heart attack. I called Jim at work to let him know and tell him the funeral details. I mentioned that I would start working on a sub for my shift at work. "You don't have to miss work. It was *my* cousin. You don't have to go if you don't want to."

Wow. That stung. Over 25 years of marriage to this man and he still thinks of things in terms of *his* family and *my* family. I have always loved Jim's family and even though he is six years older than I, we grew up only three streets away from each other, and I was friends with his sister from cross country.

"Jimmy, I am still part of the family, aren't I?" I asked.

"Of course baby, I didn't mean... "

"Well then I'm going. I'll ask my boss for the day off when I get in today."

"OK. Should we pull Grace and Theo out of school for the funeral?"

"No, I don't really think they knew that cousin very well, and I'd rather just have the two of us go."

"OK. Gotta get back to work."

The morning of the funeral was cold and slushy. The previous day's snow had started to melt a bit while the sun tried its hardest to peek through the giant stratus clouds above. Jim looked amazing in a suit. I could not remember the last time he wore a suit for anything. I was excited to see that an old black skirt I still had kicking around my closet not only fit, but was bordering on needing a belt to stay up. I jammed my wide, athletic feet into some little black pumps and hoped that the car would heat up quickly so that I could take them off for the ride.

As we were driving to the church on the south side of the city, I confided in Jim that I saw and read all 408 of his texts when I had his phone. He was silent as he stared at the road. I saw a slight flinch, but he refused to glance my way to see what I might say next. I recited a couple of choice texts that will be forever indelibly burned into my gray matter.

"Alright! Alright! Enough! I get it." he snapped. I began crying again as the texts began playing like a broken record in my brain.

We pulled into the parking lot and all I could think of was that even though he ripped my heart out, rolled it around in some broken shards of glass and shoved it back into a gaping, bleeding chest, I still actually loved him. We talked for a few minutes and he admitted that he didn't understand why I still loved him after what he did to me. That's just what the website I visited said, when it warned me not to tell my spouse that I loved him.

"How could you love me after what I did to you?" he whispered.

"I don't know. Somehow I just do." was the only pathetic thing I could find to say.

"Well, you know I love you too." With that he hugged me across the cup holders of the car and said that we had better get inside the church.

I reapplied my make up and was thankful that if anyone were to notice my puffy eyes, they would just assume it was because I was at a funeral. It was wonderful seeing all of Jim's brothers, sisters and cousins, and it was even comforting seeing his parents (although they sure did a number on him when he was a kid). But, whatever crap his dad did to him in the past was put aside for the day.

After a lovely service we all made a caravan and traveled to a little bistro near the edge of town. It was comical seeing 99 percent of the bistro packed and spilling over with people who all looked alike. I am sure it was the most crowded they had ever been on a weekday.

"Is that all your eating?" asked Mom Rohner.

"Oh, I had a big breakfast," I lied.

"Well, two pasta bow ties and a tiny salad isn't enough to keep a bird going."

"She's fine mom. We *did* eat a big breakfast," Jim lied.

"All I know is that you look different dear. Are you tired?"

"Oh, maybe a bit," I offered as more relatives approached and diverted her attention.

I was saddened by the fact that my utter exhaustion had showed up for others to see. I sure hope Theo and Grace have not noticed anything out of the ordinary. I am trying so hard to remain normal, although I am not even sure what normal is anymore.

"Hey Shelly!" It was Jim's sister. "I was sitting on the other side of the church so I didn't see you with Jimmy. I'm glad you are here."

"Are you still running much?" I inquired.

"No, my knees have been giving me hell. I'm doing some biking though."

"Jimmy and I do that from time to time, but not in the winter."

Our small talk went on long enough that I did not have to finish my wilting salad and overcooked pasta.

Next Jim's dad came over and talked to him while ignoring me, as he usually does at family functions. My father-in-law doesn't consider me real family, even after all of these years. He actually told me so one day when the twins were young. I could see that Jim was ill at ease talking to his dad for any length of time. I truly hate what that man must have done to him when he was younger. Jim should not be that awkward around his own dad. I never understood how bad things must have been and I never wanted to.

My own father was my best friend. He went to every one of my running races and cross-country meets. He always had his clipboard with the stats of the other runners on it. He would tell me ahead of time what runners I needed to try to hang with. My father even took me out of state for marathons when I was a teenager and not many people my age were running that distance. My father and I used to like some of the same music and always had a way of telling each other off-color jokes without embarrassment. We liked to burst out into song and we even loved the same foods and went on the same crazy, fad diets together.

When Jimmy's dad went back to his table, Jim's shoulders visibly relaxed and he started talking with one of the many cousins about sports and typical guy stuff. He spoke to one of his aunts about Robbie and Richie being in college, and was excited to hear that one of his sisters wanted to start running, and needed his advice on which short race to sign up for in the spring.

A dessert tray was passed to each table containing little cups of candied nuts, individual chocolates and tiny little cake pieces. As we ate, I thought about *her*. She doesn't know his history. She doesn't know the family. She doesn't know the pain his dad put him and his siblings through when they were kids. She hasn't been to the family reunions, Christmas parties or summer trips to Six Flags. She hasn't had all of the nieces and nephews over at various times for play dates. She wasn't there when Jim's sister almost lost a baby during delivery. She wasn't there when his mom had her heart attacks. She didn't send countless birthday and Christmas cards to everyone or bring over baked goods when relatives were sick. She didn't struggle with four little kids in the welfare office to collect food stamps and WIC when Jim was laid off for eight months. She is not family. I am family.

This has been my family for more than half my life. I am not willing to give that up. These are *my* memories and *my* people. If she even thought for one minute that she could just step in where I left off, then all I can say is, GAME ON!

Proverbs 14:13
Even in laughter the heart may ache,
and joy may end in grief.

CHAPTER TWELVE

In Person

*"I am human and I need to be loved,
just like everybody else does...
There's a club if you'd like to go. You could meet
somebody who really loves you."*

How Soon is Now?
—*The Smiths*

Even though it was my turn to pick where we would go on date night, I let Jim pick for the second week in a row. Once again he chose a bar with a band. It was a bar a bit farther from home with a teeny, tiny dance floor, several old pinball machines, a pool table and a few picnic tables adjacent to the bar. It looked a bit like a hillbilly bar with a moose head on the wall and some fairly weathered signs. The bathroom signs read "gents" and "dames" and there was an offensive sign that read "Liquor in the front and poker in the rear."

I started the evening with a beer, followed by more girlie drinks like "sex on the beach" and a "white gummy bear." My goal was to stick to my new limit of just three drinks, with pretzels to keep some food in me. We started dancing when I saw Hannah and another girl at the bar. I knew it was her from the Facebook pictures I creeped on. She saw me too, plain as day. Our eyes met then quickly and awkwardly looked away. At that same moment, Jim decided it was time to use the restroom. As he walked towards the john they exchanged words. I was rather quick to run over and say, "Jimmy, did you get lost?" He looked sheepishly at me and continued on to the bathroom. I waited outside the bathroom door and by the time he emerged, I was seething.

"Let's go home now," I snapped.

"Why?"

"You know damned well why. *She* is here."

"So what! I came here to have fun with my *wife*. And we *are* having fun aren't we?"

I really had to think about that one. Was I having fun? Seeing the woman who shared so much with my husband was indeed *not* fun. It was one thing to see her words on a cell phone screen, then another thing to see a few photos on a Facebook wall. Now I am 20 feet or less away from a woman who touched, kissed and who-knows-what-else with the man of my dreams.

I begrudgingly stayed for the second set but I needed another "white gummy bear" in order to get back out onto that dance floor. It was wild. At one point she was dancing only about 3 feet from us, and I literally had to turn Jim 90 degrees so he wasn't facing her while we danced. What nerve! Perhaps she was trying to make me jealous or piss me off. The little hussy achieved both goals with ease. Maybe she was just hurting in her own way because her married man was there with his wife while she was there with a girlfriend. I may never know why she chose to dance so close to us, but I will always remember the horrible pain and insecurity I felt.

Sadly, she wasn't the only flirt I had to deal with that evening. Some drunk chick was on the dance floor trying to do the "cheers" clink to Jim's glass. When he held it up to show her that his beer glass was empty, she poured some of her beer right into his empty glass. Gross. I am sure he really wanted to drink some strange girl's backwash. She was just so thrilled to be hammered on her birthday and told us so.

I began dancing a bit closer to Jim and started kissing him on the neck and making sure he had his arms around me while we danced. I wanted to make it as obvious as possible that we came as a matching set. It must have worked, as the drunk girl came over to us when we were back at the bar and said how cute we were together. Still, she did not leave and continued to talk about her birthday, and even tried to guess Jim's age. She started really low, like 35, and used that head-tilting coy thing that we girls do when we flirt. She said, "Well, I know you can't be 40 yet."

When I finally gave away that the geezer she was flirting with was actually 53, Jimmy was got mad and defensive. He pulled up his shirt to show his magnificent six-pack. "Not bad for 53," he sneered.

That was it. Fun was over. We left. I took one more look at Hannah, who was by now skank-ho dancing on some random guy's leg. I found it both crude and vulgar. Maybe I can get over her after all. In the car I was ranting and raving about how sick it is that girls flirt with him while I am with him. I did not even want to think about what kinds of antics went on all of those times when he was out with Marcus (who is nothing to look at, and has the personality of a door knob).

"You're overreacting," Jim claimed.

"And Hannah was pretty in person," I softly admitted.

"She's just a lusty wench," he teased.

"That's not funny! Why would you even say something so stupid and hurtful?"

"I'm sorry. You're right. I shouldn't have said that."

"Yeah! And what was that garbage with showing off your abs? Those only come out for *me*."

"Yeah, I agree. That was really stupid. I was just a little buzzed," he said.

"And do you know what really pisses me off?"

"What?" he asked.

"Didn't you think it was weird when we saw Pastor Gary that he gave *me* an assignment when *you* were the cheating bastard?"

Jim got very serious and his voice dropped lower in his throat. "Actually I did think that was kinda weird—but you've really stepped up to the plate. You are dancing and drinking, which I know you don't like, but I see you having fun again. You are not so uptight."

My voice and my heart softened as I very cautiously phrased my next question. "So, since I am doing something for you, would you do something for me?"

"Name it."

"Well, I took a slew of books out of the library about marriage and relationships."

"And... " he said nervously.

"Well, I think most of them are really good. We could read to each other a little bit each night and a little bit each morning before work. I think we could learn to communicate better."

I couldn't stop my motor mouth. We were in the car alone and I had his rapt attention, so I continued. "If we read a few books and nothing changes between us, then we will know if this marriage is even worth saving. I looked at one book in the library that suggested even doing a little journal entry to write things down that we are grateful for. We can take turns reading to each other like we used to do when we were first married. Remember when we used to read novels to each other?"

"Yeah, I guess so," was his ever-so-detailed response.

"By the way, what did you and Hannah say to each other when you were making your way to the bathroom?" I wanted to know.

"Actually she was kinda mean. She asked sarcastically if I was having fun."

"I hope you told her 'fuck ya,'" I said, remembering the way Jim had texted her.

As we continued to drive, I thought about why he took me to that particular bar. Did he know she would be there? He must have. Was he getting off a little bit on knowing that his two women were in the same bar at the same time (plus another one flirting with him)? It must have made his male ego soar to be the big man on campus at this stupid little dive.

I wonder what would have happened if I let the Irish side of me out on that little red head of hers. I haven't had a throw-down since junior high, but the thought of one made me laugh. I could totally take the scrawny little smoker.

I wanted to ask a zillion more questions and know many more details about her numerous texts, but I thought better of it. My nerve was wearing off with my buzz and I figured I had better not piss off the man who just agreed to spend the next several weeks reading together to work on the marriage.

At home we discovered that the kids were already nestled in their rooms, so I rushed through a quick shower and brushed my teeth. While Jim showered, I put on the best negligee I owned and was actually amazed how nice it looked after the recent weight loss. He returned from the bathroom with the exact look on his face that I was hoping for. He put on the soft night light that mimics candlelight and practically jumped into bed. The poor guy tried everything to get me to where I needed to be to complete the act, but I just couldn't get past a certain state of arousal. I wanted him so badly, and was really enjoying all of old tricks and special spots that we both know so well, but when it came time for me to climax, I just couldn't. Damn her. She was in my head. How can one pathetic woman ruin my favorite songs, my family memories and now my sex? Stupid bitch!

Song of Songs 1:2-3
Let him kiss me with the kisses of his mouth–
for your love is more delightful than wine.
Pleasing is the fragrance of your
perfumes; your name is like
perfume pored out.
No wonder the maidens love you!

CHAPTER THIRTEEN

Loyalty

*"Yesterday I lived for me, and I was so alone as I could be...
My love is a lot like me, wanting nothing less than everything...
I'll give and I'll hold nothing back."*

I'll Give
—Small Town Poets

Jimmy hit the snooze button and pulled me close to cuddle. I asked if we should start reading today and he reluctantly agreed to listen to a few pages before the snooze turned into the second warning alarm. I would love to say that these books changed our lives overnight and we lived happily ever after in a rose-colored world of rainbows and chocolate. So sorry to disappoint, but the books entailed challenges and real work. This was going to require loyalty to the marriage. Loyalty to stick to or adhere to the cause. Loyalty, devotion, duty—and perhaps more work that we had ever put into the relationship in 25 years.

We decided that we would choose one goal or task from what we had read each morning. We started off by trying to make it an entire day keeping our tempers and voices loving and kind. Epic failure for both of us on day one of what I had hoped would be the beginning of the new us. I ended up downstairs before Jimmy finished his shower, and as he emerged on the last step he said, "Holy shit! Did you see the electric bill?"

"No. How bad?" I asked as I tried not to boil.

"Those kids can't have their computers on all the time, and how much baking do you do? Is that oven on *all* day?"

"Give me a break! I haven't even been baking much since Christmas!" I snapped.

One morning after reading together, I decided that I would show him at least one unexpected gesture of kindness that day. I did a pop-in at his work, just to say "hi," and made an extra payment toward a bill of ours. That evening I had hoped he noticed the gestures and would add them to our gratitude journal. When I reminded him that I wrote my entry and asked if he would like to write his, he claimed he was too tired and would do it in the morning. Ya, right!

It took at least five days of reading before he realized that I was really putting thought into this and was serious about resurrecting the life we promised to each other years ago. I was doing my fool-hearted best to remain loyal to the tasks suggested in the marriage books. All marriages deserve the effort I was willing to put in. Was Jimmy ready to put in the same effort?

One book suggested that we make a list of what we did *not* like about our spouse. The list was never meant to be shown to the other person, but merely meant to help identify what we *did* like about the other person, by listing the negative. After Jim went to work, I got out a pen and paper and my pen became possessed. I was scared as I was able to spill out 26 things I did *not* like about him in about four minutes. I wasn't sure where I was storing all of that anger and disappointment, but there it was in blue ink. Next I set out to make the list of positive attributes, and I could only come up with nine things. Most of them were really superficial, like nice abs, soft lips, as well as a few more meaningful things like amazing father, smart and so on.

I am not sure if honesty is always the best policy, because out of fear, and wanting to keep everything out in the open for our spiritual growth, I told Jim when he returned from work that it was much easier to write the con list than the pro list and how much that scared me. I didn't read it to him or anything, but just wanted to see if he could reassure me that it was the same for him—that maybe I was a real drag, too.

My precious man was crestfallen. It was written all over his face as he told me that his con list was much shorter and that his pro list was easy to write. I was dumbstruck. If I wasn't that bad and I had some redeeming attributes after all, then why did he stray in the first place? It made no logical sense in my mind. I know he had told me that the affair was all about feeling young again. Still, my self esteem had not yet returned to its former bubbly self, and I continued to have doubts as to how this was all going to ultimately play out.

Dinner was quiet that night, as Theo had his nose in a book and Grace was exhausted from swim practice. They retired to their rooms shortly after the dishes were cleared. When one of my favorite shows came on, Jim chose to sit with me and watch it instead of retiring to his man cave, as was usually the custom. At the commercial breaks, I just *had* to ask more questions about the extent of his relationship with Hannah.

Matthew 5:27-28
"You have heard that it was said, 'Do not commit adultery.'
But I tell you that anyone who looks at a woman lustfully has already committed adultery with her in his heart."

CHAPTER FOURTEEN
The Extent of It

"Why do you hurt me so bad?
It would help me to know, do I stand in your way,
or am I the best thing you've had?"

Love is a Battlefield
—Pat Benatar

There was just no mincing of words as I turned the volume of the TV down from the remote and blurted out: "So when you and what's-her-face were alone together did you—you know—travel down south?"

Quite startled he looked at me and said, "No."

"Did she go down on you?" Holy crap. Do I really want to know this?

"Maybe twice."

"Did you guys do it?"

"We tried once. I couldn't keep it hard."

Never in my life have I felt two diametrically opposed feelings at once. On the one hand I was reeling in the pain that he tried to do the most sacred and intimate thing a married couple can do, and yet I was stifling a giggle at the same time. The words "I couldn't keep it hard" were going over and over in my head as I was thinking that maybe he had a conscience after all. That, or he was just really too drunk to get it going.

"In her texts to me she said you guys did it once. Who is telling the truth here?!"

"I am. I swear. I might have been in her for 15 seconds, but it just wasn't working."

I remained silent until he spoke again. "Why are you asking all of this stuff?"

"I'm not sure why I have to know everything. I just do. I'm still trying to figure it out in my own warped way."

"Well, don't let her get inside your head."

Too late. She's been there since I saw the first nasty text.

He confided to me that she was a level-headed woman and that they really didn't get to do too much together, as her child was her number one priority. Funny how I didn't view her that way, out late dancing in bars, but OK, we all have to cut loose from time to time. He said she was a vegetarian, like us, and that the weird thing was, under different circumstances, we might actually have gotten along.

I asked why she didn't marry the guy who knocked her up.

"He has emotional problems."

"Don't we all?"

"No, I mean he is really messed up, but his family helps her financially," he offered.

I wanted to know what she did for a living, and Jim said she didn't work. So, I was working a full-time job and an evening job while he and his sugar mama were out drinking on the psycho man's dime. Nice arrangement, Jimmy. Oh yeah, and

I had a real blast working 'til midnight at a retail store making barely above minimum wage while he and Hannah drank and danced the night away. Here comes the anger again, festering like the open, infected wound that has shaped the new me.

"I know you two were seeing each other during Christmas. Remember how all I wanted was money toward my Kitchen Aid mixer?" I prompted.

"Yeah, I remember."

"Do you remember what you really got me?"

"A purse."

"Yeah, a cheap purse for a girl who doesn't even carry purses!" I continued to ask what he got *her* for Christmas.

"I got her a workout jacket from the clearance rack of the sporting goods store," he answered.

"Oh, so she got something even better than I got. Something I would have actually used and liked," I said as I realized that he put much more thought into *her* gift.

I continued: "So she works out a lot?"

"Not like us. She's just a gym rat. She does Pilates and yoga and stuff," he said, as if he was trying to defend us. Still, I would have loved a workout jacket instead of the purse.

"I found the book she gave you," I said.

"Actually, I just threw it out. She also gave me a CD and I threw that out, too. I am trying to put this behind me. I wish you would too, Shelly," he said.

"Yeah. I wish I could."

Well, that's all for tonight, I thought. I can only handle knowing a bit at a time, and I did not want to push my luck. Jim could have just clamed up, changed the subject or retreated to his man cave. He sat with me for the whole show and even stayed while the next mindless distraction came on. Jim slipped his two middle fingers into my cupped hand the way he always used to do when holding hands. I felt the anger slip away just a little bit.

It's funny how silly little things, like the way we hold hands differently than most people, make me smile. The way he tilts his head before giving me a grin seems so much more important to me now. I hang onto those little things just in case they are the last smile, the last hand-holding or the last head tilt I will ever own.

The next commercial I spent staring at the features of his face. I know every freckle and every scar and how he got it. I know the curve of his turned up nose, his hairline, his long eyelashes, his crazy and unkempt eyebrows and even the little spot behind his ear where the hair grows in a lighter shade than the rest of his hair. I can look at his profile, shut my eyes and still see it. I had not studied such beauty in a very long time. Again I began to think, was this all *my* fault? Was I so busy with the mom and career thing that I forgot to kiss his forehead and stare into his eyes each day? I began trying to think of the last time that we really made love. The *sex* has always been amazing and prolific, but was it *lovemaking*? I wasn't sure when the last time was that we really whispered sweet nothings into each other's ear. It had certainly been a while since we had taken the time to tenderly caress each other in that endearing manner we shared when we were young.

I shut the TV off and I vowed to make my own show of real love. Taking Jim's hand, I made a gesture toward the steps. With a coy smile, he knew what I meant and followed like a little puppy hoping for a treat. I resolved to make love instead of have sex. I think it took my dear man by surprise as I spent more time than usual admiring and honoring all of his attributes. If he started to rush things, I slowed him down and told him that tonight it would just be about pleasing each other first. Poor me. I was able to please him well, but once again, I couldn't get to the place I needed to be. Damned Hannah. The anger in me boiled again as I tossed and turned, unfulfilled, throughout the night.

The next morning I added more things to my pro list as a suggestion from one of the books I was reading. I felt so much better about why I married Jim so long ago. I looked once more at the con list and got a brilliant idea. The con list was *never* meant to be shared with the spouse, but just written to get out some anger and angst. I thought perhaps I could write a letter to Hannah. I would *never, ever* have the guts to send it, but maybe it would give me a sense of accomplishment just to write it. Somehow it might make me break through a wall of healing that I had not yet been able to break through. Out came the pen and paper.

Dear Skank,

Did you really think it was okay to date a married man? Did you even for one minute consider that he already had a loving wife who prayed for him, worked hard at her jobs to help support him, respected him and helped raise the children we made together? He is *my* man to love, pray for and adore. He is *my* man to cuddle with, wake up to, take naps with and have sex with. He is *my* man to have lunch with, work out with, shop with and go to bars with.

Right now I want to rip every freaking, curly little hair off of your head when I think of your mouth on my husband's member. I'd enjoy tripping you on the dance floor and spilling my drink on your slutty jeans you wear too tight. Slashing your tires and making you pay the babysitter extra money while waiting for a tow truck would sure give me a chuckle. Speaking of your little bastard child, were you hoping to find a daddy for the little brat or do you just like giving head to men you meet in bars? And by the way... isn't your little love child from whomever quite young? Why are you out trolling around the bars on a Saturday night, and not with your kid? You're in your 40's. Freakin' grow up and take some responsibility for your child.

For that matter, honor your own gender and put yourself in any other married woman's shoes. I know you have never been married, but think about what married women feel like when our men fall prey to sluts like you. I am not saying that my husband is innocent. The fact is, you both knew that what you were doing was wrong, and you did nothing to stop it until I found him texting you the things I was already giving him. Even after you were both found texting, you continued to have contact with him after it was clear that he was not going to leave me.

Your trampy little escapades actually make it hard for me to have my orgasms. As Jimmy tries hard to get me to climax, all I can picture is his mouth on your tits. How dare you rob me of the pleasure he has been able to give me for more than half of my life. How dare you make me question my self-esteem, my body image and my overall ability to be a good wife. I will no longer give you the power to make me feel like less of a woman.

It will take Jimmy and me a long time to patch this back together, but we are both willing to work at our marriage. Sorry bitch, but 25 years and four perfect kids trumps your sad little five months of playing girlfriend to the man who belongs to me. Move on and get a freaking life. Keep away from us on the dance floor. I may not know how to dance, but I sure as hell know how to kick your pathetic, little, sleazy, ho butt any day of the week.

Sincerely,
The Wife

Proverbs 17:13
*If a man pays back evil for good,
evil will never leave his house.*

CHAPTER FIFTEEN
Convicted

*"Father please forgive me for I cannot
compose the fear that lives within me
or the rate at which it grows. If struggle has a
purpose in the narrow road you've carved, why do I
dread my trespasses will leave a deadly scar?"*

What If I Stumble?
—D.C. Talk

Wow! I had no idea what a catty little bitch I was capable of being! It felt so amazing and incredible to write that letter, yet with each word, I could hear the voice of my daddy from the grave quoting scripture to me. I remembered something from Luke about he who forgives little, loves little. Then there was Matthew 6:14: "For if you forgive others their trespasses, your heavenly Father will also forgive you." And Matthew 5:38-39: "You have heard that it was said an eye for an eye and a tooth for a tooth, but I say to you offer no resistance to the one who is evil. When someone strikes you on your right cheek, turn the other one to him as well." I really hate that one.

It is so humbling for a competitive person like me to fathom doing nothing. I just really want to see her suffer the same gut-wrenching pain I must now live with. Does she know what it is like to just crumble up into a little ball and just cry until your abs hurt? Can she see that all of my memories of the love Jim and I had or have are now forever tainted?

Romans 12:17-18 says: "Do not repay anyone evil for evil; be concerned for what is noble in the sight of all. If possible, on your part, live at peace with all." And Ephesians 4:31-32 reminded me that: "All bitterness, fury, anger, shouting, and reviling must be removed from you, along with all malice. And be kind to one another, compassionate, forgiving one another as God has forgiven you in Christ." I had forgotten that one, but when I looked it up I knew immediately that for my own healing, I had to write another letter, as difficult as I thought it was going to be.

Dear Hannah,

My heart was broken into a million pieces when you texted my husband that you wanted to be in his pants that Friday night that you and Jimmy knew I would be working late. When all of the heartache, sadness, anger, and frustration subsided temporarily, I realized that there were not one, not two, but three of us at fault.

I may have thought that I was helping the family dynamic by working extra jobs, when in fact I was enabling Jimmy to go out and play. I was always tired and unemotionally available. Jimmy and I just sent two of our four children off to college, and we are only four years away from being empty nesters. He must have been feeling old, and admits that part of his attraction to you was that you made him feel alive and young again.

As for you, I am sure that having a child in your 40's with no husband can be daunting. Using Jimmy to feel secure and loved was almost understandable. I am sure he was wonderful to Tyler, as he has always been a fantastic father to our four angels.

I know he cared for you deeply. I guess I am writing to let you know that I am letting go of the blame, the shame, the feelings of inadequacy and the anger that try to control me on a daily basis.

I forgive you. I pray that you find a lovely, single man who is just dying to be a great father to Tyler. I thank you for reminding me to take care of my husband. I will enjoy and relish each and every moment we still have while in this physical life.

God bless, and stop smoking for Tyler's sake.

Now I really mean it when I say...

Namaste,
Shelly

Well, I guess that wasn't as hard as I thought it would be. I put both letters inside the journal I kept in the room I use as an office. I felt momentarily better, but knew that sometimes total healing just takes time. The rest of the week dragged on and on, as silly things like song lyrics could still set me off fairly easily. While out for a run (with the iPod that Hannah had given Jim, freshly loaded with songs from *my* library), I heard the Anberlin song "Inevitable" where they belt out in a soulful, sad way "I wanna be your last first kiss, that you'll ever have..." It sent me right over the edge again. I realized that I was no longer Jimmy's last first kiss. Hannah was. Now I know that it is over between them and Jim and I have kissed many times since then, so technically I *am* his last first kiss, but it's just not the same. He kissed her within the boundaries of our marriage. Marriage: the ultimate union between two people. Marriage: the joining of two people as one. It is still so raw. It still hurts so much.

Four miles later and back at home I decided to text the pastor. I asked why I still felt so much anger after I thought I had appropriately forgiven Jim and Hannah. He texted back that anger and forgiveness are cousins, and he confirmed my own suspicion that it will just take more time. He suggested that Jim and I come in for a follow-up session when we have the time.

Back at home I showered and began dressing for date night. I chose black jeans and a white camisole. Over the camisole I wore a short-sleeved, peach top with sparkly beads. Jim came into the bedroom as I was looking for my boots and confessed that he had done a long run with intervals. We were still going on date night, but he warned me not to expect too much action later, as he anticipated being tired from the intervals. I asked him where the band was that he wanted to see this week.

"The Peach Tree Tavern," was his response. That was a classy joint much farther from the other two places he had been taking me. I remembered that we had gone there over a year ago with Marcus (the door knob), when Marcus was still married to a woman named Donna. Marcus didn't like dancing any better than I did at the time, so we sat at a little round table and watched Jim cut the rug with Donna. Now that I came back in the picture for date night, Marcus stopped calling Jim, cold turkey. I guess now that he's divorced and Jim is tied up with me, Marcus felt he lost his wingman. It sure is nice to know who your real friends are!

We made sure we knew where Theo and Grace would be for the evening, and got into the car. The drive was pleasant as we stumbled across a new radio station that played a lot of the college radio songs, with few commercials. We arrived, but before the valet took our car, I just had to ask Jim if he had ever taken Hannah to this tavern.

"No, why?"

"I just wanted to know that at least *one* bar could be considered *our* bar."

"Oh, Shelly, *every* bar is *our* bar!"

Believe it or not, that was only the beginning of a night that will go down in my memory as a classic. The valet took our car and Jim held the door for me. He sauntered up to the bar and ordered the first round of drinks for us. The place was packed so we wedged ourselves into a corner by the dance floor and placed our drinks on one of the round tables. A group of four came up and asked if they too could rest their drinks on our table.

As we made small talk with the couples, I noticed the exquisite, crystal jewelry on the taller of the two women. We began talking about her neighbor who makes and sells the jewelry. With that statement, Jim pointed to his wedding ring and said, "This is the only jewelry that *really* matters." He shot me a big grin full of pearly whites as he squeezed my hand. Later when he pulled me to the dance floor (yep, he still has to coax me out there), he stared at me for what felt like minutes at a time. Usually he peeks at me to see if I am having a good time, then scans the crowd or watches the band perform. Tonight it seemed, he only had eyes for me—and I was loving it.

The best part was that I knew there was no ulterior motive for sex, as he had previously warned me that he would be tired later. So he was just staring at me because he chose to. He was just smiling at me because he was happy. He was just holding my hand because it felt good. It was the first time in a long time that I felt truly cherished and truly adored. A girl can get used to that kind of high.

During the break, Jimmy and I went out to the alley that attaches the inside bar with the outside patio. He pushed me right up against the wall and planted tender kisses on me that tasted better than milk chocolate. My heart was racing like a lovesick teenager and I wondered where this pitter-patter feeling had been hiding in me all of these years. Most of the night was like that… kissing, dancing and smiling. I talked him into staying for all three sets, hoping the fairy tale would never end.

Proverbs 16:24
Pleasant words are a honeycomb,
sweet to the soul and
healing to the bones.

CHAPTER SIXTEEN
Fairy Tales Do End

"*Can you hear the sound of my heart break
with each step you take?
Can you feel? Can you feel me when I say
please come back to me...
All I am, all I have is yours to find.*"

Please Come Back
—*Michelle Tumes*

I don't usually consider myself to be premonitory, but the fairy tale ended the next morning when I answered the phone.

"Hello?"

"Yes, is James Rohner there?"

"Yes, can I ask who's calling?"

"Well, this is Bart from Sam's Fitness and I wanted to know how he enjoyed his free trial membership. Was he interested in joining?"

I forgot my filter again. You know, the thing that every mouth and tongue should come with? I forgot that Jim might walk downstairs while I was talking to this bozo. I forgot that Grace was in the next room signing onto her laptop.

"No! He is *not* interested in joining. He was only using that place to meet his little girlfriend. This is his *wife!* I don't think we will be joining at this time."

I tried to remember if Bart was the same salesman who tried to coerce me and my friend Noreen into buying a membership. I sure am glad that I had lied about my last name and phone number when I visited.

Slam! I almost chipped a nail hanging up the phone with that much force.

"Mom! What was that all about?" came Gracie's concerned voice from the other room.

Think fast Shelly, think fast! "Oh, I was having fun with one of those annoying telemarketers," I replied. God, I hope she bought that.

Jim came into the room and announced that the weather was getting nice and he wanted to take Grace and Theo to his favorite part of our state park and camp from Saturday night to Sunday. Just a quick overnight that would allow them to have special time with just dad, and maybe give me a chance to go out with my friends.

"Why don't you call your friend Mary? You haven't called her since she and her husband moved to the west side."

"I'm just feeling kinda blue. I may just stay in tonight and catch up on sleep. We were out rather late last night," I reminded him.

He pulled me into the other room where Grace could not hear the rest of our conversation.

"Ya know, I would feel better if you didn't mope around the house. I heard the phone call and I know why you are upset.

Honestly, you know that it was over a month ago that I went there with her. That's all behind me now. You know that."

"Yeah, OK... whatever."

Jim told the children that he would pack the car while Grace was at swim team practice. I began packing a cooler for them and Theo rounded up a few books to take with him for the trip. Theo can do the outdoor thing for a while, but enjoys reading by the campfire the most.

It must be great to be a guy. Men can just compartmentalize things so well. They can just put on their work hat, then their sneak-out-to-see-the-girlfriend hat, and afterward come home and screw the wife. They can live in the moment and turn their thoughts on and off like the kitchen faucet. They can see their wife break into two pieces on a phone call, then just get up and take the kids camping on the spur of the moment!

Women on the other hand have to think about stuff and agonize over it. We have several thoughts going on at one time, which isn't always a good thing. It sucks to be thinking of the grocery list, watching your son play in the band concert and still have *her* permeating your thoughts. It stinks to be at the grocery store deciding on which new herbal tea to try and then see a curly red head in the aisle. It may not be *her*, but it then makes me think of the whole five months of my life that I was oblivious to anything out of the ordinary. People make blanket statements like "Oh, a woman always knows when her man is cheating." Well, no, they don't, and I am living proof of that.

I was cheated on. I was lied to. Yes, omission of the truth is also a lie in my book. I am trying so hard to be normal and put this all behind me. It simply isn't that easy knowing that somehow, in some way, I did not measure up to keeping Jim faithful and loyal to me. How is it that I had no idea? Am I the exception to the cliché?

Much of the rest of the day was spent with the iPod on and the super sad, depressing songs washing over me like a tornado leveling a small neighborhood. I knew Jim was right about getting out of the house for a bit, so around 5 p.m. I started making calls to friends.

I called my friend Mary but she and her husband already had plans. I called one of the few single friends I had but she was busy too. I finally got my friend Joni to go out with me. We decided on a cheap place in town for a meal and then we'd see if we felt like going anywhere afterward. Dinner was nice and I almost told her about what had been going on with Jim and his little mid-life crisis, but I just couldn't. I still felt so humiliated that I was not enough for Jimmy and that somehow he had to go somewhere else for some sort of fulfillment I could not give. Joni, a divorced woman, several years younger than I, made the night a bit more exciting when she shared some of her escapades with men she had been seeing off and on. "In fact," she said, "I told Ben I might see him up at the bar later when the band plays."

Oh boy. We ended up back at the bar that Jimmy first corrupted me the night I was instructed by my pastor to lighten up. The band was actually really fun. It was a grunge band that I know Jim would absolutely *hate*. Joni had friends all over the bar who were buying us drinks. I knew my limit and made sure I would stick to my usual two to three drinks, possibly four if we were eating food. I had not dressed in anything special. I had on jeans, a black T-shirt and my pirate boots. I barely had any makeup on. Why would I get all gussied up for a night with the girls? Still, this short but cute gentleman with a full head of wavy hair was checking me out, and I think I actually blushed! He came over to me, saw my wedding ring and asked if I was *happily* married. I smiled, tilted my head and said, "I am afraid so."

"Damn. I just had to ask." And with that he walked away.

"Did that dude just talk to you?" Joni asked.

"Oh, it was nothing."

"Then why are you blushing like a seventh grader?" she teased.

"He asked me if I was happily married, and I am." At least I *was* and hope to be again someday.

"Shit, Shelly. You could at least dance with him if he comes back over here. It's just a dance."

That's where she was dead wrong. There is a really corny song I used to listen to called "Slow Fade." It is based on the Biblical principle that you should never put yourself in a position of temptation. If you don't want to do drugs, don't hang around druggies. If you don't want to be fat, don't work at a fast food dive. The words alone convinced me that I should be doing something more worthwhile with my Saturday night. "Be careful little eyes what you see. It's the second glance that ties your hands as darkness pulls the strings." Such apropos lyrics for my night. Still, for Joni's sake I stayed and danced some more.

By the second set I noticed that I was dancing differently than when I dance with Jimmy. I was somehow more free. I moved my arms more and spun around. Was it the band? They were playing some of my absolute favorite S.T.P. and Pearl Jam songs. I assumed it was, because I had no one to impress and I just danced as if no one was watching. Well someone was watching all right. The short guy with the wavy hair came up to me again and started dancing in my space. He even bumped hips a bit into mine to the beat and whispered in my ear, "Such a shame you are married. Ah, the things I would like to do to you." With that he had even worked his arm around my waist a little.

I recoiled faster than Usain Bolt on speed. Yikes! Gross. I did not even want to imagine another man's paws groping me. To taste anything but Jimmy's soft, milk chocolate flavored kisses would turn my stomach. To look into another man's eyes would be a betrayal of the greatest magnitude. Still it was a rush to feel good-looking enough to attract the attention of another man. Is this what Jim feels like all the time when he goes out and the women flirt with him? I now know that it will be a cold day in hell before Jim goes out without me hanging on his arm! I stormed over to Joni.

"Joni, I think I should leave. Do you see Ben yet?"

"He texted me a while ago that he isn't coming. Why do you wanna leave?"

"I think I have a creeper, and he is making me feel weird."

"One more song and I promise," she said.

Eight songs later we were on our way home.

Sunday alone was really long and lonely. I still had Jim's phone so I texted Theo to see if the kids were having fun with dad. They were. I Skyped the twins and only got Robbie in his dorm. He saw what my mother-in-law had seen at the funeral.

"Mom, you look tired. Your face is really thin. You OK?"

"Oh, it must be because I miss you so much," I laughed.

"Well, I talked to Richie and his last final is a day before mine so a guy from his dorm is going to drive him here and we will come home for break together!"

"I can't wait to have us all together again," I said, trying not to let the tears well up.

"Hey, put Theo on the webcam."

"Theo and Grace are with dad having a day of camping."

"Remember when he took just me and Rich? I got lost on the hike and he *freaked out!*"

"Oh, I remember, because we did not have cell phones and the park ranger had to call me to tell me that they had found you. I didn't even know you were lost, but the ranger assumed dad had called me!"

"Yeah, and then after dad had freaked, you freaked in overtime."

"So glad you were found. I sure could use a hug right now," I said as the tears were now evident.

"Mom, we'll both be home soon. Don't cry."

Don't cry. I have been telling myself that daily for what seems like an eon. Each day is filled with memories of our love, our family and the trials and tribulations I have endured being a mother of four and a wife to the most reticent man I know.

I spent the balance of the afternoon going through all of our photo albums and copying all of the photos of Jim and I kissing each other. I put them into a separate scrapbook with little notes about where and when they were taken. I dug around until I found some old journals I had written when we were young and saw that we really were the *same* people... just older. I still like going out. He still likes movies. I don't mind drinking every now and then. He still likes having a romantic meal in the dining room once in a while. I don't mind watching a Clint Eastwood film if I know that I get good couch cuddles from it. We both still like running. We both enjoy a good book. We can still make each other laugh. The fact is, no matter how hard this hurts, I still love that man too much.

I vowed to make it a point to make new memories and new photos of us kissing each other and add them to the scrapbook. Maybe this whole stupid episode was put in my life to shake me up, shake me to the core and give our marriage a fresh start. Such a shame that it couldn't be done without all of the agonizing pain, the tidal waves of tears, the loss of appetite, the lies, the feeling of being used, the fear and paranoia I now face and the fact that I still can't get my mojo back in the bedroom.

When the campers came back, they looked pleasantly tired and very dirty. Spring at a campground can be very muddy. I offered to start the laundry and pulled a quick bread mix out of the pantry as the water filled the laundry machine. Grace came in the kitchen to help me and Theo was very talkative. Even Jim seemed refreshed and renewed.

"I missed you babe," he said as he worked his arm around my waist and kissed my neck.

"Missed you too."

"Did you go out with Mary last night?" he asked.

"No, Joni and I went out."

"Joni? Holy crap. How much did you drink?" Ah, he knows her well. "Or should I ask," he continued, "how late did you stay out?"

He laughed as I told him that we were there a long time waiting for her male friend to show up and he blew her off. We both remembered the time we went out with her years ago and she got so hammered that we stayed until we knew she had a safe ride home from a mutual friend. She is my reminder that, as much fun as it must be to be single, having a constant in my life is nice too. I was not going to mention the creeper who tried to dance with me, but remembered that omission of the truth is just as bad as a lie.

"So this guy tried to dance with me even after seeing my wedding ring. I didn't let him though," I said.

"Well I should hope not!"

At that moment, the laundry tub had filled and I made my escape to put the first load in. Back at the kitchen table, I showed Jim the scrapbook I had started with all of the kissy pictures of us when we were younger. It was really fun taking a walk down memory lane. With digital cameras being the norm now, I don't even know if we have real photos of us recently or just files on the kids' cameras that we somehow retrieve and print out. I like the real photo albums that you can touch and feel. Call me old-fashioned, but I need my photos in chronological order, and in an album as well.

"These are great photos, Shelly. I forgot how thick my hair used to be," he commented.

"Did we ever get the last Christmas pictures in the family album?" he continued.

The last Christmas? I really want to forget that one. I bought a ton of awesome things for Jim as I worked so many extra hours at the retail store. I really went off the deep end with nice clothing, workout stuff and another season of sitcom DVDs. All I got was that crappy purse. "Oh, I'm not sure. I'll have to check on that later," I answered, hoping he would forget.

The week went by faster than usual, as I was called in to work a couple of extra days. Hoping that work would be a great distraction, I jumped at the extra hours. We stayed in that weekend as the boys came home from college and we all wanted to catch up with tacos and ice cream. The whole family even agreed to wake early and go to church as a family. After the service, we encouraged the kids to get some cookies in the great hall of the church while we tried to corner Pastor Gary before his next service.

"Pastor, can we set up that second meeting?" I asked.

"Sure. I am thinking Tuesday or Wednesday evening. Just set it up with the secretary," he said as other people were approaching him to comment on the great sermon.

Back at home Jim put the college radio station on and the perky little DJ that mistook me for Hannah was on. It brought a whole bunch of memories of dedicated songs back to the forefront of my thinking. Jim read both my face and body language.

"What now?"

"I'm still trying to figure it all out. Exactly *what* did you have with her?"

"What she and I had was *nothing!* It doesn't even compare to what *we* have. No comparison! I am over it. It was wrong and I knew it was wrong." He pulled me close and took my head in his hands. Looking down at me, he kissed me and reached around for a long hug. I questioned why I even brought it up. As he let go of me, he changed the station to the one we found by accident the night we drove to the Peach Tree Tavern.

Psalm 28:2
Hear my cry for mercy as I
call to you for help,
as I lift up my hands
toward your most Holy place.

CHAPTER SEVENTEEN
The Phone Call

"Flies in the vasoline we are.
Sometimes it blows my mind.
Keep getting stuck here all the time..."

Vasoline
—Stone Temple Pilots

Despite all of the love, security and great date nights Jim was treating me to, I still continued to have what I call "tidal waves." I would appear perfectly normal, functional, happy even, and then this tidal wave of sadness would knock me down. The only thing that would get me out of it was to go and have a good cry into my pillow that Jim had won for me at an amusement park a few years ago.

I run on the treadmill or venture out into the rainy spring and run until I am spent. I listen to sad love songs in some feeble attempt to know that I am not the only one feeling this pain. I try to appear happy and normal for the kids, but I am still not eating like I used to. I mope around. I don't enjoy going to work and faking a smile. I follow my husband around from room to room when he is home, as if I still need to see what he is doing every waking minute. My pathetic mind is still thinking that if he is spending the time with me, then he can't be spending it with her or anyone else.

I still have Hannah's number memorized from all of the snooping I did when this all blew up in my face. Do I call her? Would she clear up any remaining questions I have? I decided to text her from my own cell phone.

it's shelly. 4 my own healing, would you b able to talk?

2day is my b-day. u can call 2morrow, she replied.

I never realized how long an afternoon could be. When I did call her the following day, I thanked her for taking my call. My first question was to ask her if she had ever seen Jim cry.

"Yeah, he has cried for me," she answered rather casually.

Was it about the stuff his dad did to him or about stuff I did to him?

Neither.

Crap! Why didn't I have the nerve to ask what he cried about? Chicken shit, Shelly! I wanted so badly to know what made his giant wall of emotions come down for *her* when it never comes down for *me!*

Next question: "Why did you put those disgusting, dirty songs on the iPod you gave him?"

"I know you are a religious person but I did not think they were disgusting. They were either songs I liked or songs we heard when we were out together."

Out together. Out together. Out together. No matter how many times I hear that in my head, it never sounds OK. I felt as if a thousand bees had just stung me all over. The word "liar" was all I could think of. "Fuck You Like an Animal" and "Crazy Bitch" were *not* songs that they would have heard at the bars they frequented. I know my Jimmy well enough to know that he would have never liked any grunge or heavy metal.

OK, move on. Don't call her a liar to her face. Just finish the call. I basically told her how much I did not understand why he did this to me while I was being so good to him, loving him, working extra jobs for him, and staying in great shape for him. I admitted that I would have almost *expected* something like this 15 years ago when I was fat, tired, running after four babies and taking care of aging parents. All she must have heard was that I called myself fat. She told me not to have such a negative body image. She admitted that when she was with Jim she really didn't think about me at all. Nice! How thoughtful.....not!

"I know what we did was wrong, and I will never do it again to you or to anybody. I hear all of my girlfriends' drama. Guys are pretty much all assholes. I hope you guys are getting out together more," she said.

"Yeah, we are. Thanks for talking to me. I'll pray that you find a really nice man who is dying to be a daddy, too."

"Thank you."

"Goodbye."

"Goodbye."

Even though I was calm on the phone, I was shaking as I hung up and deleted the record of her phone number from my cell. A dozen or more questions popped into my head now that the call was over. Why didn't I write down all the stuff I really wanted to know ahead of time? Did it matter? In the end, it was now up to me to move on. Did this phone call help me or make it even more real hearing her voice?

Worse. Definitely worse. I felt like I just took one step forward and two steps back. Wishing I had asked her more questions consumed the rest of my day. I don't know what I was thinking. Was I thinking that we would become friends or something? That thought made me sick.

I made the call to the church to set up our second meeting with Pastor Gary and played on the Internet to find a new gingersnap cookie recipe. Trying to distract myself with baking, I made three different batches but it really didn't help much. By evening TV time, I was a wet dishrag. I just sat at the couch and stared at mindless show after mindless show. Jim picked up on that right away and when we were out of hearing range of the kids, he asked me what was up. There was no way I was going to tell him that I was so insecure that I actually called Hannah and talked to her!

"I really don't know why I just can't get her out of my head!"

"Well sweetie, if she is in your head, then *she* wins and *we* lose."

Why didn't I think of that? Jim and I have always been competitive. When he put it in terms of winning and losing, it made sense. I am allowing her to win. I am allowing her to get in my head and ruin all of the work that we have been putting into rebuilding our marriage. Lately Jim has shown me nothing but hard work. He has removed the temptation of the cell phone, he spends more time with me, he is willing to go to the pastor, we are reading excerpts from various relationship books, and our communication has been more open and honest. It's no longer Jim who has to change but me. What is holding me back?

"Pastor said he can see us again on Wednesday and see how we are getting along," I mentioned.

"Cool. What time?"

"Right after work if that's OK."

"Sure. Maybe if it's still light outside, we can go for a run together," Jimmy offered.

The Phone Call

Wow. Jimmy take a slow day for me?"Sounds great," I said.
Wednesday arrived without fanfare. I skirted around telling the kids where Jim and I were going and told them just to reheat what I had made for dinner. This meeting with pastor was much shorter, and he seemed distracted and quick to get us out of there. I later found out that someone close in the church family had died suddenly, and that he had many counseling sessions set up back to back for the family members.

"So how have things been going?" he asked of us both. Jim just stared at me and I have to admit that I am tired of always starting the ball rolling. I just looked right back at him until he decided to speak.

"Well, I think we are doing well. Shelly is going out more and quit her evening retail job. Now she has more time for us," he offered.

"And Jimmy doesn't use his phone. We are trying to do more things together but I still feel really insecure all the time. I know he doesn't like me following him around and telling him I love him all the time, but I don't know how else to really let him know that I *never left him!* I have always been there for him if he just looked," I blurted out.

"Are you taking turns deciding on date night?" pastor asked.

"Well, I let Jimmy pick most of the time because it makes me happy to see him happy." Yuck. Did I just sound that sappy and insecure? Yes. Yes, I did.

I brought up the subject of Theo's trip with the school jazz band. I know Jim had no real desire to take perfectly good personal or vacation days to go, but the pastor strongly suggested that Jim go with us this year. Jim agreed without hesitation, but as it is my job to over analyze everything, I felt like that was the pastor's way of saying, "Don't leave Jimmy home alone for a weekend just yet."

I continued to tell him how Jim listens to and reads parts of the many relationship books I took out of the library and that we are trying many of the suggestions together. Pastor Gary seemed impressed at the length Jimmy was going to move the relationship forward. He also reassured me that this whole event will take more time to heal. He told Jim that he was doing the right thing by answering all of my questions openly and honestly. He acknowledged that these truths will hurt me, but will ultimately help the trust issue if honesty is in place. He admitted that his own wife can tend to over analyze things, but that it is just the way women are wired, and it is an attribute to be revered and not feared. With that, he sent us on our way and apologized for the brevity of the meeting.

At home Jim lived up to his promise of running with me. At first I felt great running with the man I used to run with back in the day. Soon after we were up our street, however, he started pulling ahead and I was already feeling the heavy breathing coming on. I felt ashamed to ask him to slow the pace a bit, but he did willingly and we ran close to three miles before I told him to just go on ahead.

The celebration of Easter was lovely with all four kids. Jim and I had been getting along so well. For a few days I actually thought I was done thinking about my misery. Then, there it was, a sick feeling one morning when I awoke. Another tidal wave of fear and sadness overtook me. I asked Jim a few questions I had asked him before, and got the exact same answer. Was I trying to catch him in a lie? Was I hoping that the answer would be better than the first time I had asked it?

"Honey, I wish you could put this behind you. You can cry if you want to, but Rob and Rich are going back to their schools soon and I just want to have a nice day with them before they leave," Jim said.

"I'm sorry. I have no control over these waves. I thought that they were getting more infrequent and that they were not even waves anymore—just puddles. I am so sorry."

"It's OK. Michelle, I love you." He never says that without me saying it first. That felt wonderful to have an unsolicited "I love you." I wish all men knew how important that is for a woman to hear and to hear often.

We spent the morning in the kitchen with the four children, a plate of buckwheat pancakes and a fruit salad. We talked, laughed and finally had to say goodbye to the college boys until summer. Richie had a ride from a friend, and Jim drove Robbie back. I insisted that he take his pay-as-you-go phone back in case he needed it on the way back from dropping Rob off.

"Are there any minutes left on it?" Jim asked.

"No clue, but please put some minutes on there in case of emergencies. Have a safe trip."

"I will."

"Oh, and don't think I don't know that you get to take a night off of reading our books. We start up right away tomorrow night!" I reminded him.

"Oh boy," he said, as he rolled his eyes.

Colossians 3:14
And over all these virtues put on love,
which binds them all together
in perfect unity.

CHAPTER EIGHTEEN
Lessons in Love

"The words I have to say
may well be simple but they're true.
Until you give your love,
there's nothing more that we can do."

Love Song
—Elton John

The challenges from our recent readings proved harder than we both expected. Jim hated the forced time before bed and in the morning before work, but it was the only time that we did not have jobs, errands, workouts and kids to deal with. He often asked if we could just skip a day here and there. I was firm in my resolve and trudged onward. Many nights I would cry my eyes out and Jim always questioned if the books were even helping if I was always crying. Yes, they really were. These relationship books took the rug we were sweeping issues under and shook it out. It took those marital dust bunnies out from under that rug and made us face them head on. We were confronted with the realization that we took a lot of things for granted. We forgot how to talk about anything other than bills and the kids, and our tastes for music, entertainment and things we liked to do together had changed a little bit. We even realized that we spoke different love languages. I only felt love when Jim spent time with me and we never had that with the many part time jobs I was working. Jim only felt love when I was affirming him with words and nice gestures. I guess I gave most of that to the kids and forgot to pay attention to Jimmy as well.

One day we talked to each other about forgiveness. Naturally, Jim asked me to forgive him for stepping out with Hannah, which I said I had already done. It was now my turn to ask him to forgive me too. He seemed a bit confused on that one.

"What do you have to ask me to forgive? You didn't do anything," he queried.

This was my big chance to tell him in a super nice way that I had been an enabler for years and it got me nowhere. In fact it allowed him to go and play around with a red-headed demon. I looked him straight in the eye as we were sitting on our bed. I grabbed both of his hands and made sure he was listening and making clear eye contact with me as I spoke.

"I want you to forgive me for emasculating you."

"What do you mean?"

"For years I have jumped in and tried to fix things. If the twins needed new soccer equipment or Theo wanted to get his own trombone, I would jump in and take on more jobs. I did odd jobs, retail jobs, night jobs and anything to bring more money into the home in order to keep afloat. I never let you be the man of the house, the provider, or the head of the house that you were meant to be. I just saw what *I* thought was a problem and went out to fix it. We really didn't need brand new stuff all the time. We needed each other. We needed time together. We needed more time at the dining room table as a family. We needed me at home more to be that helpmate that a good wife is supposed to be. Instead I was addicted to working, and it all just backfired in our faces. Will you forgive me?"

There was a long pause as Jim was taking in the onslaught of words that I just discharged. "Well... I admit that I let you do all those extra jobs so I didn't have to," he claimed.

It felt wonderful to me that he admitted what I already knew. I needed to hear that from him, and I continued to tell him that I was down to working just one job now and that all I wanted was to be home more for the remaining two kids and to be a better wife. Would he forgive me for enabling him all these years? It may be hard cutting back our income level a bit, but you can never get back quality time.

"So do you forgive me?" I asked again.

"Yes, Shelly. I forgive you."

Another day I asked Jimmy to just say a prayer for me and that I would say one for him too. Naturally we would share what we prayed about. I was so excited that he chose to pray for two of the three things in my life that I did not know he even knew I was interested in. He prayed for me to get back into my baking hobby as a little business and he prayed for me to have a great garden. Maybe he knows me better than I give him credit for.

That same evening I decided to make a fabulous dinner for him. I set out the china we use for holidays and dug up some half used candles. I wanted to make sure it was going to be a fun evening. I made one of Jim's favorite meals of vegetarian chili and cornbread. I lit the candles and had Average White Band on the CD player by the time I heard the car in the drive.

I was pumped. Although he noticed the candles and china, to my dismay he gobbled down his food in about 11 minutes and left the table while I was still savoring the meal. Normally I would have let him, but something told me that if we were going to hold nothing back and be totally honest with each other, then I had to tell him how I felt.

"Seriously Jimmy? I am still eating!"

"Oh, yeah—I'll sit with you."

The conversation was phatic at first and then progressed to more informational things that really mattered to the two of us. We relaxed and just enjoyed the moment. I brought out chocolate cake with a coconut frosting and we talked some more.

After several weeks of reading, Jimmy seemed to understand that perhaps this was helping me and he stopped complaining and making excuses not to read with me. He even put a few entries in the gratitude journal at night. One book in particular began delving into loving even if it is not reciprocal, another mentioned dealing with lust versus love, praying through areas of wrongdoing, and a third book looked at ways to help meet the other one's needs. I was most impressed with an article I came across on a Christian blog site. It talked about leading the heart versus following the heart. Often *following* the heart can lead to lust or something forbidden. The phrase "We had an instant connection" ran through my head as I realized that when Jimmy and Hannah felt a connection, he should have *led* his heart back to me instead of *following* what may or may not have been a true connection.

Learning how to include your spouse in your future decisions and future successes was a good lesson for us, as in the past we just went to our respective jobs, put our fun money into our own accounts and just pooled enough money into the joint account that we would need for the bills. When I wanted something like new running shoes, I just went out and got them. When Jim wanted a new lounge chair for the man cave, he just went out and got it. On this night, we talked about running all purchases over $100 by each other first.

"I mean, it's not like I'm going to tell you 'no' on a purchase, but even if it is something that is mostly for you, like the lounge chair in the basement, I would still like to feel good about being included in the decision," I claimed.

"Yeah, I guess I could do that," my man of few words responded.

"I know when I need stuff for the kids, because I am around them more, but I guess I should still ask you about expensive things they want and need before I rush out and get them," I offered.

"I would like that because maybe I could even help you find it cheaper. I mean, we probably could have saved a lot of money buying a used trombone for Theo last year."

"I agree, sweetheart," I replied.

Wow. *Real* communication like a *real* couple. It was amazing as many more similar conversations began to fill our time together.

As we rounded the time to renew the library books again or purchase the most favorite ones on Amazon or eBay, we decided to write a letter of commitment to each other. I was able to pen mine easily. Jim on the other hand had to be poked, prodded and eventually begged before he finally wrote it over a week and a half later.

Mine read:

Dear Jimmy,

I will try to keep this short, as I have already written volumes on why I love you, how I love you and how I will ALWAYS love you... no matter what life throws at us, and no matter where we end up.

It began back in the '80s as just a few beers with a really cute vegetarian I met in a bar. You know, a physical attraction (*eros* love). And then we got to know each other better (*phileo* love). Maybe we got stuck there for a while raising our kids, but in the 25 years (28 if you count the time we dated) we have been together I have seen many sides of you. Ugly sides. Mean sides. Selfish sides. Hurtful sides. I have also seen loving sides. Funny sides. Endearing sides. Sweet sides of you. These are the sides of you that make it a blessing to continue to love you as I love my own self. I *choose* to love you. Now THAT'S **agape** love. My promise to you is to love you unconditionally from here on out.

Please commit to me, as I have committed to you. I know it won't always be easy to love me. But I can guarantee that I will make it worth it.

I love you with all of my heart and all of my soul.
Shelly.

Jimmy's letter to me read:

Dear Shelly,

I hereby commit my love to you forever. I will do my best to give you the love you deserve to have from me, and the kind of marriage we both need. I promise to spend more quality time with you, help you out as much as I can and cuddle you more.

Love you,
Me

Even though Jimmy's letter to me was short, I knew that just putting that on paper was a big step for him. I tucked his letter into my journal and knew that we were on our way to putting this mess behind us.

Theo came home from school announcing that he was one of the band members selected to go on the high school tour. I knew that if he was accepted last year that he would most likely be asked to go again this year, but I tried to act appropriately thrilled that he was "selected."

"Oh, that's fantastic Theo."

"Well, I figured they would pick me, but now it is official," he smiled.

"When does the money have to be in?" I asked.

"I think by the end of the week. Here's the info. Are you going to be one of the parents that goes too?" he asked.

"Well, I think even your daddy wants to go this year. You OK with that?"

"What? That would be friggen' awesome."

"Watch your language. I never like to hear young men saying friggen' and freakin'."

"Sorry mom."

A thought just came over both Theo and myself at the same time, and we both burst out laughing as we said simultaneously: "What about Gracie?"

Within minutes, I was on the phone to one of Grace's favorite friends, asking her mom if their family wanted another daughter for a few days. All it would entail was them having

Grace sleep over and take her to school on Friday and swimming on Saturday. After working out the logistics of that, I went for my run and hoped that Jim was sincere in wanting to go with us on this trip.

Colossians 3:20
Children, obey your parents in everything, for this pleases the Lord.

CHAPTER NINETEEN

Jazz Night

"Could it be that everything is sacred? And all this time everything I've dreamed of has been right before my eyes?"

Sacred
—Caedmon's Call

I wanted Jim to have the best possible experience for our mini vacation, so I spent a fair part of the week making various mix CDs for the long car ride. I wasn't concerned with what kind of music Theo would want to hear in the car, as he would be tuning us out on his iPod or reading. I made the first CD of mostly what I call "Jimmy rock." This included songs from Creedence Clearwater Revival, David Bowie, Eric Clapton, Jimi Hendrix, The Kinks, Led Zeppelin, Neil Young, The Rolling Stones and so on. Next I made one to keep us awake with songs from Lady Gaga, Jessie J., Madonna, Mary Mary, and anything techno. Naturally I had to have a '80s/'90s CD with Morrissey, Simple Minds, Depeche Mode, Thompson Twins, The Psychedelic Furs, New Order and the like. I had a decent grunge CD with Pearl Jam, Stone Temple Pilots and

Nirvana songs for me as well as one romantic CD with Luther Vandross, Average White Band, Enya, Out of Eden, Prince, Seal and Phil Collins.

We started the drive early, and followed another family until the second rest stop when they wanted to surge ahead. Jim and I decided to do a 10-minute jog around the parking lot to stretch out our backs. Theo slept a lot and it allowed time for Jim and me to just talk about anything that came up.

"I was thinking that I could start baking again for families that are too busy to bake. I was thinking about setting up a website to send people to with my catering fees and information," I stated.

"How much will a website cost?"

"Some are practically free. First I need to come up with a catchy name and nothing rhymes with Shelly other than smelly," I lamented.

"Maybe it doesn't have to rhyme. Maybe just something simple like Shelly's Delights or Michelle's Bake Shop."

It was adorable to hear Jimmy helping me with my ideas instead of just grunting. He shared his disappointment with me about things that were going on at his own job. Being at a small company, they could basically jerk him over on dental and insurance plans. They also stopped any opportunities for overtime and had not given raises of any kind in over a year. I had no idea what was going on there, as when I usually asked him "How was work?" his response was always "Work is work." I felt privileged that he was finally sharing something about the place where he spends 40 hours of his waking week.

The stay at the hotel was wonderful. The students went off with the band and orchestra leaders for practice, and Jim and I enjoyed a workout at the hotel fitness center. We were able to run side by side on the treadmills at our own paces. Next he lifted weights while I stretched my lower back and did a few yoga poses. Dinner was wonderful too. He never bitched about the menu prices, and seemed excited talking to Theo about the pieces the children would be playing. Was he having fun? It sure seemed so.

The main concert day was quite long. There were other schools performing, so we watched when we had to and then went outside for long walks and even took a short nap in the car. Theo's school had a stellar performance to my untrained ears, but I was glad to get back to the hotel and just relax.

Back at the hotel, Theo went to hang out with some of the other musicians in the lobby, while Jim brought out a travel-sized Mancala game. He admitted that he had not played in years, so we took turns sharing my reading glasses and deciphering the directions. We played a game, but we were convinced that it should not have taken that long to find a winner.

"Let's look up strategies on You Tube," I suggested.

"You can do that?" he asked. Jim only uses the computer when he wants to find the best price for something. Even then, he gets one of our children to search it first then show him how to do basics like scroll up or down to see more.

"Sure. I'll show you. Just go to the You Tube website and type in the search bar what you want to watch."

"Can you do that with porn?"

"Ha ha, Jimmy. That's all we need to be watching when Theo comes back in the room!"

"Just asking," he teased.

We found a whole series of videos with various strategies and decided to play again a few times to try them out. I must say that it was one of the most fun, non-sexual times I have had with Jim in years. I was ashamed of myself for being surprised that I could have non-sexual fun with my own husband.

The next day there were more concerts and more time alone with Jim. I loved being hours from home and hours from all of the issues that had been haunting me. As the day went on, I found myself becoming depressed. I think I was scared that when we returned home, we would just start grunting at each other again and forget all about the laughter at Mancala and the fitness center workouts. At the hotel for the last evening, we called to check on Grace and packed as much as we could for leaving the next morning.

"Hey, wanna watch a movie? We don't get all these movie stations at home."

"Yes, Jimmy. I am well aware that we are the only people on the planet who don't have cable, or satellite."

"How about this?" he said as he flicked to some blood and guts action film.

"Give me that!" I said as I snatched the remote.

I found the old movie "When Harry Met Sally" with Billy Crystal and Meg Ryan. We had only missed the very beginning, so Jim conceded to watch it without rolling his eyes. I had seen the movie at least four times but had forgotten about all of the little interruptions in the movie where they have these little interviews with old married couples. The interviews had an underlying current: The couples with most successful marriages felt that they had fallen in love at first sight or felt that they had married their best friend.

I had never really thought of Jim as my best friend. He started out as the hot guy at the restaurant. Next he became the boyfriend, and later the boyfriend that ran races with me. After that he became the husband and the father. I always used my girlfriends to play the best friend role, but perhaps that was one of our problems. I asked Jim a few choice questions as the movie ended and another romantic comedy was about to run on the movie channel.

"Jimmy, do you remember the first meeting with Pastor Gary when you said I was judgmental?"

"Well you can be," he said matter-of-factly.

"I know, and I have been working on that. But I guess what I am saying is that I secretly thought of *you* as really judgmental too. Isn't that weird that we see in each other the stuff we don't like in ourselves?"

"I never really thought about it, but I guess so," he replied.

"Who is your best friend, Jimmy?"

"I don't know if I have one."

"Well, I feel a lot more open and honest with you now that so many issues have been brought up by the books we read and the talks with the pastor."

Jim knew I had more to say so he just kept listening. "So, I think maybe that's why we got so distant from each other. We started thinking about each other in terms of spouse, parent, bill payer, worker and not best friends."

"Well, we sure tell each other everything now," he said with a chortle. Next he said: "Well, at least I tell *you* everything you ask."

"Yeah, I know I've been really nosey about everything. I swear I'll get over this eventually, but in the meantime, can I try to be your best friend?"

"I'd like that," he said as he kissed me.

We left the next morning and Theo and Jim seemed thrilled to be back home. I was still nervous that being back home meant back to reminders of the affair and back to the old grind.

Also, now that we were done talking to the pastor and had finished most of the relationship books I took out of the library, would we be able to keep progressing on our own?

Philippians 4:6-7
Do not be anxious about anything,
but in everything, by prayer and petition,
with thanksgiving, present your requests to god.
And the peace of God, which transcends
all understanding, will guard
your hearts and minds in
Christ Jesus.

CHAPTER TWENTY

Jealousy

*"Though you know it's only jealousy,
you can't help but be haunted by your passion."*

Possession Obsession
–Hall and Oats

Jim and I went to The Peach Tree Tavern one evening. We were there for dinner and hoped to see a new band we had never seen before. Jim ordered a simple pasta dish and I just ordered humus and chips. As we were enjoying our first beer, one of Gracie's school teachers came in with his wife. Jim noticed first, and pointed them out to me. I made some silly comment about the teacher having dreamy eyes, and he got all bent out of shape about it. At first I laughed it off, as he and I always look at the gorgeous women in the bars and even comment on things like crazy big breasts or ridiculously long legs. I thought nothing of saying something about nice looking eyes on the male teacher. When I saw that Jim was incensed about my comment, I went to the bathroom to cry. When I came back, he was gone.

When we were very young and maybe only married about three or four months, we were quite insecure and stupid like we were behaving tonight. Jim being absent was definitely something I did not expect at this juncture of our lives. So, I sat at the table for at least 10 minutes. I knew that he didn't go home without me, but was more than likely sulking in the car.

Sure as I know my Jimmy, he came back inside a few minutes later and announced, "I'm leaving. Do you want a ride home?"

"No, I wanted to stay for the band. Please stay for the band."

"I don't want to."

I was pleading by this point, and determined to move on. He begrudgingly stayed for part of the first set, but he refused to dance. Now this was beyond weird that I was the one wanting to dance and have a good time and Jim refused to get up from the table. With that attitude, I decided that we had better go home.

The ride home was totally silent and very long. When we got home, we started up again with yelling and shouting about the comment I made.

"Can you say double standard? Shit, Jimmy! How can it be that it is OK for you to stare at other chicks' boobs and long legs but I can't say that the school teacher has dreamy eyes?"

"Why don't you just sleep down here tonight," he said, referring to the couch I had slept on for years.

"No. We are over that. I want to figure out why you are over reacting like this."

He had had enough going around in circles with the argument, and gave me a nice shove down onto the couch. I rose and shoved him back. He rushed toward me again and I put one arm up over my face to protect it and grabbed the back of his shirt with my other hand. I tore and pulled at the shirt but have no idea why. My hand had a mind of its own. He put his right hand on my throat and pushed me up against the wall hard. Even though it appeared that he could choke the hell out of me, a certain calmness enveloped me. The thought occurred to me that even though he had the power to choke life from me, it would still be a better kind of pain than the pain of imagining him naked with another woman.

He quickly released my neck and we let the "F-bomb" go off a few more times as we yelled at each other. I followed him upstairs. I knew that Grace and Theo must have heard us arguing, but I prayed that they did not hear what it was about. In the bedroom I kept asking why it was OK for him to look at other women and even date one behind my back, yet I could not appreciate another man's eye color.

"Well, now maybe you know how insanely jealous I can get over you!" he said.

"I guess I should be flattered, but it still seems like a double standard," I retorted.

"No, it's different than when I see a pretty girl in a bar. There is no emotional connection. With you and Mr. What's-his-face, there is a connection. You see him at school functions and you know him."

"Well you sure got to know Hannah!" I whispered angrily.

Our bedroom is in between both kids' rooms, and I really had to watch what I was saying out loud. "Not fair. Are you going to throw that in my face forever?" he asked.

"You *broke me* Jimmy. You even said you had a *connection* with her. How could you? How am I supposed to ever get over that? It will never go away. Even though I forgave her and forgave you, I still have all of this anger raging in me."

"Let's just go to bed. I'm sorry I overreacted," he said as he pulled down the cover and the sheet.

Just like the comments about me being judgmental, I felt that this whole night was about him seeing in *me* the ugliest side of *him*. Did he really think I was capable of having an affair simply because some other man has nice eyes? For Pete's sake, he should know me better than that.

As I tried to sleep, I came up with an idea that I thought would help. The next morning I slipped out of bed as quietly as possible. I was on a mission to do some sorting and organizing of all of the journals and diaries I had been keeping off and on throughout my life. I ran across one that was when the children were young and all of our parents were requiring our attention too. The first entry was a Bible verse.

James 1:2-4 *Consider it pure joy, my brothers, whenever you face trials of many kinds, because you know that the testing of your faith develops perseverance. Perseverance must finish its work so that you may be mature and complete, not lacking anything.*

I laughed to myself reading that verse. Wow, I guess I am not lacking much now, I mused. If I can get through *this* agony, I'll be golden.

Inside that particular journal was a declaration that I was determined to stay in the marriage no matter how insignificant Jim made me feel. I also found some nasty notes we scribbled to each other when we used to argue and then not speak to each other the next day. I didn't bother to save the mundane notes that said things like: "Don't forget to get the twins to soccer today." But I did save all of the hurtful notes like: "Don't bother coming to bed. I'll take care of things myself," or "You selfish son of a bitch. I can't do it all!"

I went back up to the bedroom with the journal. I placed it on the table by the bed and crawled back in next to Jim. He was awake, and rolled over to face me. "Sorry about last night," he said apologetically.

"Me too. I'll try to stop throwing Hannah references at you."

"OK."

"So, I was sorting and I found this old journal from when things were *really* awful with us. Remember when I was running ragged with all the kids and you were still racing and hanging out with your friends a lot?" I asked.

"Where are you going with this?" he worried.

"Well, I was thinking how I shouldn't have all of these negative things lying around the house. I'd actually like to have a burning ceremony."

"What's that?"

"Well, it's where you take all of the things that you no longer want to define you, and burn them. We could put my ugly purse you gave me last Christmas in there and the letter you wrote me the night I caught you texting, and all of these horrible notes we wrote to each other from years ago."

"Jesus, why did you save all of them?" Jimmy wanted to know.

"Truth?"

"Yes, truth!"

"Well, at one time I thought that our marriage was so bad, that I saved the notes thinking that if we ever did get a divorce, I could use these nasty notes as evidence that you were selfish and I was the one working extra jobs, taking care of kids and checking on our parents all the time," I answered.

"Did you hate me that much?" he asked softly.

"It wasn't hate, but just a stress I had not ever dealt with I guess. I don't think I am capable of hating you."

No response as Jim rolled over to turn away from me now. He was hurt and did not want to look at me. I climbed out of bed and crawled in again on the other side to face him.

"Jimmy, I know it was stupid to hang onto all of this stuff. I think that's my problem now. Let's just go out back and burn it all by the fire pit."

"It's supposed to rain today. Maybe tomorrow," he said as he rolled over to face away from me again.

"Tomorrow" dragged on for a couple of weeks. There was always an excuse not to have our little ceremony. I assumed that he trivialized my pain by putting this off day after day. One morning I came downstairs and blew up at Jim for no apparent reason. I am not sure what possessed me, but I somehow made it about the affair. Jim continued to make his lunch for work while I bitched and moaned about him not understanding my pain and about him being incapable of change. I stormed out of the house and walked down to the garage. I picked up the first thing I saw (a broken skateboard) and flung it at the garage. I found a few pieces of wood, and an old plastic chair and began throwing them as well. Not ready to come in yet, I plunked myself down and began babbling and babbling to myself (or God) about him not being the man I expected him to be. What a revelation. Here I was wondering when *he* would change when perhaps *I* was the one who needed a change as well. What must it be like to be Jim, always walking on eggshells and wondering when the next tidal wave of tears (or in this case rage) would pop up in me? Maybe I was also expecting him to fulfill all of my needs when that is not really his job. Do I love him more than God? Do I put him before God? Do I expect Jim to be everything to me? I have a lot to think about on my next long run.

I came back into the house and tried to smooth things over before we both had a crappy day. Later that evening, we lit a fire. I read each and everything out loud one last time, and we vowed to never treat each other with such disrespect ever again. It felt good to see the letter and all of the mean spirited notes go up in flames. I even burned the ugly purse from the Christmas that I lived in ignorance.

We stayed at the fire pit for a while longer, and shared a beer while listening to the boom box Jim had brought out. We tried to find the new radio station we liked so much, and marveled at how they played so many songs in a row that we *both* liked. When all was said and done (and burned), Jim peed on the fire to extinguish it and we returned to the house.

I thought to myself how good that felt to put away the bows and arrows of nasty words we used to fling at each other over the years. I know we will still fight and bitch about things that are ultimately pointless in the grand scheme of things. We are human, after all. Still, I felt like we had *both* won something tonight.

Exodus 14:14
The Lord will fight for you;
you need only be still.

CHAPTER TWENTY-ONE

Summertime

*"Give me a soft subtle mix, and if it ain't broke
then don't try to fix it.
And think of the summers of the past."*

Summertime
—Will Smith

One weekend we decided to spend Friday night with the kids. Robbie and Richie were finally home for the summer. We decided to eat out and see a movie at the second run theater. What a great night. Everything felt so normal. I almost had an entire day without thinking of *her*. This was *my* family and we just had a picture perfect evening. When Jim and I retired to our room, we made love, and for the first time in a long time, I was able to go to that special place that had eluded me since seeing her in the bar that first time. Maybe I was going to be normal again after all.

The next morning was unusually hot for so early in the summer. We asked the kids if they wanted to go bike riding. A resounding "no" came from all four.

"How about driving to the beach?" Jim offered.

"I hate sand," Gracie said.

"I have to coach at CYO," chimed in Robbie.

"Maybe we could just hike in the state park," I suggested.

"Too hot," Theo answered.

"I'm tired," whined Richie.

It was hard to face the fact that one glorious night as a family was all the kids could take for now. Jim looked at me and said, "Well, I'm not wasting a gorgeous, sunny day."

"Same. Let's just do something without them," I suggested.

We decided to pack a picnic basket of pretzels and apples, our suits, a few beers, two camping chairs and the blow up inner tubes. We drove close to an hour to the lake at the state park and poured the beers into a plastic container in case the ranger was cruising the beach. We spent close to four hours there, alone. I made a rule that just for the day it had to be about just us and that we had no kids.

"Did Robbie ever tell you how much he is making doing the coaching job this summer?" Jim asked.

"Robbie who?" I giggled.

"Oh… yeah."

A few minutes later he commented: "You know, our kids are lazy. I can't believe they didn't want to *do* anything today."

"What kids?" I reminded him.

He finally got the message that we were pretending to be young and childless again, so he blew up the inner tubes and pulled me into the freezing cold water. The temperature of the lake was way behind the scalding sun of the midday. We lounged for a while until my bottom, which was hanging down inside the tube, was almost numb. Back out on the sand to warm up, we drank our beer, munched on the pretzels and relaxed. It was the first time in a while that I did not feel the need to force the conversation, ask questions about Hannah, or bring up bills or issues about the kids. We just sat and enjoyed the silence.

I stared at his beauty the way I did the night Jim sat and watched TV with me at the beginning of spring. This time I started at his feet. I observed his hammer toes with the cute little tuft of hair on each one. I admired the length of those runner thighs and the sandy hairs that were trying to peek out of the top of his trunks, just below his belly button. His abs were still rockin' like that of a man in his late twenties, and his chest was sculpted well from the weight training he does during the winter months when he can't run as many miles as he would like to. He rolled onto his left side as I rolled onto my right and we locked eyes. No words were spoken. No words had to be. It was just us, and it was just glorious.

"Well, I'm hungry for something more substantial than pretzels and apples. I guess we should get going," he later announced.

While Jim squeezed the air out of the inner tubes, I picked up the pretzel bags and shook out the sandy towels. I tossed the apple cores into the bushes for the park critters to enjoy and folded the camping chairs and followed Jim to the car. As we drove up the winding road leading from the parking lot to the park exit, I fiddled with the radio looking for a good tune.

"Hey! Put it on *our* station." Jimmy said, referring to the new station we stumbled upon the night we went to The Peach Tree Tavern.

Our station. The words rolled around in my head for a while as I played with the knob. I smiled to myself thinking that he and Hannah had a few songs that were *their* songs, but Jimmy and I... we had a whole freaking station!

We stopped for some ice cream at a little stand outside of the park. We savored eating it in the parking lot, instead of the usual rush of eating while we were driving. Maybe Jim wanted just a bit more time together before the rigors of parenthood consumed the rest of our day.

At home I showered to get the sand out of my hair, while our mutual friend Todd called, and asked if we were going to see the '70s band Jim liked so much. We had already been out the night before with the kids, but if we budgeted the amount of money we would spend, I thought we could swing going out two nights in a row.

I knew the band Todd was referring to was playing at the bar where we usually have what we call "it" sightings (the bar where Hannah hangs out). I needed to look simply amazing, so I found the black jeans that lift my flat rear end up a bit and chose the purple, sleeveless top that makes my shoulders look amazing. I borrowed some eye shadow from Grace that made my brows sparkle a bit, and even played with foundation powder to give the appearance of a slight tan. I begged Jim to wear the Lucky Brand jeans that sculpt his butt and are a bit tight on those athletic, runner thighs.

Todd arrived earlier and we saw him in line to pay the cover charge. We cut over to where he was and entered while there was still free popcorn. Jim and I were at the picnic table munching away when he excused himself to go to the bathroom.

"You're not going to talk to any pretty girls on the way there are you?" I teased. With the most gorgeous smile, he replied with "I'm already talking to a pretty girl!" Good answer, Jimmy.

"It" arrived later than usual, and I noticed that she appeared somewhat smaller. Now, I don't mean that she lost weight or wasn't wearing her heels. I mean, she just didn't give me that same visceral response. My gut was OK. My self-esteem? Check. My confidence to dance with my husband? Check. She was smaller in significance to the role she played in my life. I wondered if it was because Jim and I had recommitted to each other with our letters or if it was just time that was beginning to heal me.

Later I saw Hannah touching and resting her head on a tall man with a preppy shirt and a protruding pot belly. I won't lie. I felt a bit smug as I thought about how I get the six-pack, the toothy grin, soft lips and milk chocolate kisses while she may end up going home with the paunch.

I thought I felt my cell phone vibrate so I looked down at it and saw Theo calling. Knowing that I would never be able to hear over the loud music, I went out to the patio where the smokers go to light up. All Theo wanted was to ask if he could leave Grace alone and sleep over a friend's house. As I hung up another couple was texting on their phone and smiled my way.

"Checking in on teenagers?" I asked.

"No, the babysitter." The woman replied.

We began a conversation of small talk and as we were chatting, the girl Hannah often arrives with came out for a smoke. She was sort of on the outskirts of where we were talking and seemed to be listening in. As the couple went back into the bar, the girl came over and announced that she was Hannah's best friend. I really had no idea what that had to do with anything but I simply stated that I had figured that already.

For whatever reason, this woman, (Abby) felt the need to talk about everything from her own Jewish faith to the fact that Hannah was a really good woman and not a slut. She told me that she really cared deeply for Jim and that they only did "it" once.

"Ya, I know. Jimmy told me. In fact he told me he couldn't keep it up for her," I said smugly.

"He never could with Hannah," she said, "because he loves you," she finished.

That was very healing for me to hear. She went on to talk about everything and anything pertaining to those five months, and it was a real relief for me to hear that everyone got their stories straight. Everything she said was the same thing I heard from Jimmy as well as Hannah, herself. The one thing Abby said that should have hurt me, but didn't, was that Hannah did *love* Jim. She told me that Jimmy just didn't know how to reach me or let me know what he needed or something along those lines. Man I wish I hadn't had those drinks so I could have remembered the conversation word for word. In the end I guess it really didn't matter.

Jimmy had started missing me by this point and had emerged from inside. He looked shocked that Abby and I were chatting it up. I assured him that I was fine and I even grabbed Abby with one arm and Jimmy with another and gave them a big, drunken hug before going back inside for the next set.

In between the second and third set, Todd left to check out another bar. We walked him to his car and then sat in our car deciding whether or not to go back in for the last set or just call it a night. I was feeling so strong. I can only ask Jim questions about Hannah when I am having a strong day.

"I know you don't throw the word *love* around easily, Jimmy, but you texted her that a few times. Did you love her?"

"I don't know," he continued. "It really bothers me when she is here."

"Why?"

"She's a bit of a monster," he said.

"A monster? What do you mean?" I asked.

"What she did to our family."

Wow! I felt like tonight the shoe was on the other foot. I was feeling great and yet he was feeling crappy about the last several months. As far as I knew, the kids did not suspect anything and so I had not even thought about how it may have subconsciously affected the *whole* family. Jim may have been feeling more guilt than I assumed. My father always told me that assuming something makes an "ass" out of "u" and "me." Maybe when Jim sees her, it is a reminder to him that he stepped out, and that he was vulnerable and dishonest and that he followed lust instead of love. Those are definitely emotions that can bring down an evening.

"Yeah Jimmy, but we *fixed* it," I said, referring to our marriage. I added "Most people just divorce, walk away or even get revenge when there is cheating."

My man of very few words came through for me. "Only the *stupid* ones don't fix it."

With that statement, he fired up the Oldsmobile and drove home with one hand on the wheel, and the other hand working his middle two fingers into the middle of my semi-closed palm, in that special way that we hold hands.

2 Corinthians 4:8-9
We are hard pressed on every side, but not crushed;
perplexed but not in despair;
persecuted but not abandoned;
struck down but not destroyed.

CHAPTER TWENTY-TWO

Our Anniversary

*"Sometimes it's hard to follow your heart.
Tears don't mean you're losing. Everybody's bruising.
Just be true to who you are."*

Who You Are
—*Jessie J.*

Summer came and went all too fast. Jim and I entered a relay race where we each had to do a 5K. There was a couples' division and we won it. The victory was much more special than if we had each entered as individuals.

One morning, after reading together, we set a goal to do some out of the ordinary things for each other over the next few days. One day I asked Jim to help me in the garden. Usually he just does the tilling in the spring and leaves the rest to me. On this day, however, he learned the names of some of the plants I planted earlier in the season and helped me weed for nearly an hour. On another occasion, he talked me into donating blood with him. This is something he does on a regular basis, but I have never done it, as I abhor needles. When Jim saw an article in the local paper that there was a critical need, he asked if I would go with him.

"They say that one pint can save three lives, Shelly."

"You know how many needles I had in me when the twins were born? I have never liked needles," I replied.

"I'll sit with you if you like," he urged.

"OK. How long will it take?" I asked.

"Well, I can fill a pint in just under seven minutes, but it's not a race," he teased.

So, he and I gave blood together. We gardened together and we raced together. We were still going out once a week, yet with our 26th anniversary coming up I found myself in more than one card aisle, unable to purchase a card for him. Things were going so well with us, but knowing that last year at this time he was about to be unfaithful to me made me sorrowful about *this* anniversary. Last year I was so excited about the goofy grin and the lovely kiss he planted on me when we renewed our vows, but then one short month later he gave his heart away to a total stranger. It seemed sort of hypocritical to me. Nope. I just couldn't get a card. Instead I went home and typed him a letter.

The morning of our anniversary was sunny but windy. I went for a run before work and came home with a scratchy throat. I just missed Jim leaving for his job, but kissed Grace and Theo before they both went off to high school. It was weird knowing that my baby was entering high school but also a relief knowing that Theo would watch out for her and show her the ropes. He was driving the two of them as I jumped in the shower.

After work I picked up some wine and came home to check on the dinner I had thrown into the Crock-Pot earlier. I had just enough time to make muffins before Grace and Theo came back from school. Jim came home from work and immediately went for his run as Grace started picking at the muffins.

Dinner was lovely and I enjoyed hearing the banter of the kids talking enthusiastically about their upcoming year of high school. Theo was preparing to take the SAT in November and Grace was thrilled to be trying out for the high school swim team. Official practices would also start in November.

After dinner the kids retreated to do homework, and Jim presented me with an anniversary card. I opened it cautiously. It was a large, lovely card with a red foil heart on the front that read: "Today is the day I speak from the heart… " On the inside it stated " …and my heart simply says I love you." It was signed "Love, Me" but Jim knew better than to put the little XOXOs on the bottom. He remembered that one night when I cried miserably telling him how much it hurt when he texted XOXO to Hannah. I told him that those two letters were now tainted and I never wanted to see them written to me ever again. Still, I missed seeing them at the base of the card. Be careful what you ask for!

I tried to thank Jim with sincerity, but the tears were already welling up in my eyes. "I am so sorry, Jimmy," I cried. I handed him the letter I had typed and walked away.

Dearest Jimmy,

I am so sorry that I just couldn't get you a card this year. I know that it has always been our special tradition. I tried… more than once. I would be at the store looking through the cards, and all I could do was wipe away the forming tears. I love you so much it hurts, but I keep thinking about last year when we renewed our vows in front of all of those people. You gave me a really personal, wet and long kiss in front of everyone. There were more people at our anniversary party than at our real wedding and that sweet kiss in public was so personal... as if we really had a "connection."

Then, less than a month later you made a "connection" with another. You shared things that were so deep and personal with her... things you did not even share with ME! I know this because you allowed me to text her when you were trying to end it and then later we actually talked once on the phone.

While I was blindly thinking that things were great between you and me, clearly they were not. While I was begging for dates and eye contact you were giving those things to another woman. While I was giving you everything from romantic lovemaking to nasty ho-sex, you were thinking about her. I can't even fathom the idea that you used to come home on a Saturday night LONG after Saturday Night Live was over and make love to me... perhaps with her cigarette breath still on your lips. In fact, I think I just threw up in my mouth thinking about it!

I know that you have seemed to put this all behind you. I am so jealous that you guys can turn things "on" and "off" like a sink faucet. Thank you so much for picking ME and deciding to save our very long and precious love for one another. It just isn't that easy for me to get over the fact that no matter how many jobs I did, how well I performed sex, how good of a mom I tried to be, how many degrees or certifications I got, etc... that it just wasn't enough for you and you needed to look for more than I could offer you. It hurts knowing that I wasn't good enough, and that I may never be truly what you are looking for or are satisfied with.

I guess I need to take the whole year to work this out in my little, insecure brain. Yep, a whole year. You see, this year when I have my birthday, I will be remembering that last year you were sneaking around trying to see her. When Christmas comes, I will think of the nice workout jacket *she* got as well as the fact that all of those winter "hikes" you took were really excuses to go and see her and her toddler.

New Year's will be the WORST, as I remember the texts about how bored you were at the New Year's Eve Party. Was it really just "same old-same old"? I know you were busted texting her in late-January and you continued until mid-February, so maybe by the end of this February I will have suffered enough and we will have made enough NEW memories of all of the holidays I missed last year.

I know that I am breaking the request you had for me to stop dragging up the past and for that I am truly sorry. It is who I am. Call me insecure, stupid, paranoid, ridiculous or whatever you want, as they are all most likely true. Now that I have this off of my chest, please help me to heal by continuing to give me all the things you have been promising me for years... more eye contact, more quality time and more hugs. I don't need money, status, fame or glory. I need your physical and emotional **_spirit_** each and every day. I love you. I cherish you. I adore you.

Sincerely,

The Wife who never gives up on our love but who is still hurting

Later I was reading a book in bed and Jim came up and climbed onto his side. He made no comment about the letter. Yep, that's my Jimmy. Keep it all locked up inside. He made no gesture and no attempt at anniversary sex. The next morning I found the letter in his trash.

We never spoke about the letter. We were both busy keeping up with Theo's band schedule, Gracie's swim schedule and making those never-ending college tuition payments for the twins. Still, the lines of communication were more open than they ever had been, and I continued to journal my feelings to try to keep the tidal waves at bay.

Fall was rapidly approaching and I became nervous as the days got shorter. Jim has been known to have a bit of a temper when the weather forces him to work out indoors instead of in the sunshine. In the past the kids have made cracks about him having seasonal affective disorder, but there is always a bit of truth in teasing.

To my delight, this fall was exceptional. Jim was irritable from time to time, but we began talking about issues at his job or situations with our kids as they came up. I worked hard at rerouting bad vibes. I guess the enabler in me came out sometimes, as I would often go out of my way to keep the peace.

"Are you kidding me? You went shopping and forgot bread? What the hell am I going to make my lunches with?" he screamed one day.

"Well, I have to get Grace from swimming, so I'll leave early and get you some, love." I said, hiding the anger from the unsolicited attack. When I returned with two different loaves of bread and a smile, he was a completely different animal.

Another time he accused me of running the dryer too long and wasting electricity. I peeked in the dryer and saw that it was filled with Grace's swim towels. It wasn't even me who had used the damned dryer, but I took the fall to keep the peace.

When the snow was still deep, a friend pulled into the drive and tore up the grass a bit. When we had a warm day and he saw the ditch in the grass, his first reaction was to blame *my* driving. When I told him who it was, he actually apologized for accusing me without asking.

I continued to be grateful for the fact that these mini-episodes were just little pimples on the face of our marriage and that they were truly few and far between compared to what I now call "the ugly years" when we snapped at each other for the slightest provocation.

Keeping the energy level in our home more positive was not as difficult as I had imagined, and perhaps it is true, you *can* catch more flies with honey than with vinegar. And oh... the honey can be so darned sweet!

Romans 12:18
If it is possible, as far as it depends
on you, live at peace
with everybody.

CHAPTER TWENTY-THREE
The Holidays

*"I lost at love before. Got mad and closed the door.
But you said, Try, just once more."*

You've Made Me So Very Happy
—Blood, Sweat and Tears

Theo and I practically share a birthday. We usually celebrate together, and this year was no exception. We planned for a family dinner at a restaurant that serves the best veggie pizza in town. Theo and I shared a black olive, onion and green pepper pizza, while Grace and Jim shared an artichoke and spinach pizza.

Grace has been known to be quite generous with the Parmesan cheese shaker, and Jim started the teasing right away.

"Hey Grace, why don't you have a little pizza with that Parmesan cheese?"

"Very funny, dad."

"Can we trade one piece each?" Theo asked. I was thrilled that my picky eater was willing to try the artichoke and spinach.

While Jim was trading pizza slices with everyone, I asked if we were going to have dessert here or go home for the cake I had made yesterday.

"All I have to do is throw the icing on the cake I made yesterday," I commented.

"I want ice cream, too" Grace chimed in.

"Jimmy, we'll have to stop at the store first. We don't have any ice cream. I forgot."

"I didn't," he said. "In fact, I bought ice cream and a bottle of wine to share with you when we get home," he announced.

Back at home we watched Theo get the typical teenage gifts of iTunes cards sent from Robbie, a nice card from the ever-broke Richie and a new book from Grace. We scored big-time by getting him a Kindle.

I was just about to open my gifts when Jim announced that I had to open *his* gift first. It was a lovely silver Italian charm bracelet with one single charm on it. The charm was a little mixer whisk to represent my obsession with baking things. I now understood why he wanted to go first. The other children had gotten me a running shoe, a Jesus fish, my birth stone and an "M" charm to go on the bracelet. It was lovely, and I was thrilled that Jim must have taken the time to secretly coordinate all of this.

"We should Skype the boys and thank them for the gifts." Jim said.

"Yeah, I want to tell Robbie about some girl in my class who is still asking about him," Theo laughed.

"When are they coming home for Thanksgiving?" Grace wanted to know.

Only Robbie was in his room when we called, so we texted Rich and called it a night. In bed I felt only a twinge of melancholy as I tried to be secure in the fact that I had gotten through another holiday where new and better memories were made.

"Do you wanna make love?" Jim asked.

"Do I have to?" I teased.

"I am all about making some new memories my dear," I said, fully knowing that he had no idea what I was talking about.

Thanksgiving was amazing. The first snow of the year came right as we were sitting at the table to pray. It had been raining before, so the trees were picking up a shimmery sparkle from the snow freezing all of the water. Norman Rockwell could not have painted the picture any better. We served the traditional Tofurkey fake turkey with all of the other accouterments like pumpkin pie, stuffing, veggie gravy, mashed potatoes, sweet potatoes and cranberry jelly with my fresh baked rolls.

When Jim announced that he wanted to go for a hike to work it all off, I believed him. It sure helped that Rich went too, though. The remaining kids and I cleaned up and decided to get out the Christmas decorations and put on the Christmas music. Knowing the older boys had to go back the following day for three more weeks of school made it OK to put up the decorations so early.

The phone rang and it was Jimmy's brother Trevor. He wanted to speak to him but when he heard Jim was hiking, he just decided to dump on me instead.

"Man, Shelly, you and Jimmy really have it made. I just signed the divorce papers with Monica and now we get to fight about all of the shit we need to get rid of or argue over."

"The papers are final?"

"Yep."

"Can I ask you a personal question? You don't have to answer if you don't want to."

"Fire away."

"What happened to you two? You always seemed so happy."

"Didn't Jimmy tell you? The bitch was cheating on me!" Trevor spat.

"Oh," was all I could muster up.

"I mean, I have forgiven a lot of crap from her, but some things are just unforgivable," he snapped.

"I guess so," I lied.

"I mean, I gave her everything—a nice home, a nice car, jewelry. We had mutual friends and I thought we had it made like you two."

"Oh, we have our ups and downs too," was all I alluded to.

I wanted to tell him so badly about the situation with Jim and me, but I knew that if Jim wanted his brother to know, it would be his job to tell him. Trevor continued to talk until he had gotten it out of his system and all I could tell him as we hung up was to keep the faith. What does that even mean? I was so bummed after the call. Why are we such a throw-away society? Why do we give up on relationships so easily? Where is the loyalty in this world? What's worse is that I should have at least tried to give him a few good Bible verses or asked if he had a favorite pastor to talk to. Maybe I felt that since the papers were already signed, that it was a done deal. I wish I would have known earlier that they were having problems and I wish I had mustered up the nerve to share my faith.

When Jim returned from his hike with Richie, I told him about Trevor's call. He confided in me that two people at his work just filed for divorce in the last year, too. I was thinking about one of Grace's teachers as well. She had called to tell me about how well Grace was doing on a project that her class was working on. She somehow worked into the conversation something about being a single mom.

"What is wrong with everybody?" I asked.

"People are too quick to give up I guess."

"I'm glad we didn't—ya know—give up."

"Me too," Jimmy said as he flashed me the smile I live and breathe for.

Jim sat at the kitchen table as I served us the second piece of pumpkin pie of the day and poured a cup of coffee for each of us. I took my fork and swirled the whipped cream around the top of the pie as I enjoyed the quiet reflection of the fact that we did stay together. It made me think of a sermon that Pastor Gary had recently preached. He was talking about the cliché people use when they know you are suffering some sort of pain. Friends are quick to say "God only gives you problems or situations that you are strong enough to handle." Pastor Gary told us that that statement is crap. Yes, our pastor used the word crap in church, but did so to prove a point. He went on to explain that God does not give a person cancer, He does not cause you to lose your job, He does not put your teenager on drugs, He does not run your credit card up, or in my case God did not put Hannah in front of Jimmy and set up an affair because He thought I could "handle" it. If God had preordained every horrible event in our lives, then we are just puppets that He controls. God gives us the freedom of choice to do stupid things like overeat, do drugs, get into debt, have affairs and so on. He knows we will mess up, but it is our faith in God that gives us the strength to turn around these situations and heartaches.

"Jimmy?"

"Ya."

"Thanks." I said.

"For what?" he asked as he put way too much sugar in his coffee.

"For going to church with me even though it's not your thing, and for understanding how important it is to me."

As I savored the last flaky crumb of pie crust, I said a silent prayer of thanks to my deceased father, Earl, for giving me the perseverance and faith that he learned from his parents. I can remember rolling my eyes at all of the corny stories he told me when I was young and I never understood half of the Bible verses he quoted. Now, as an adult, they have served me well. He really knew what he was doing by setting such a stellar example of a Godly man to me and my sister. After placing the dishes in the sink I began thinking about the next holiday.

Christmas was around the corner. I started making out the Christmas cards and I got this absolutely crazy idea to send a Christmas card to you-know-who. I was not going to put a return address on the envelope, but I did sign it. It was just a run-of-the-mill, generic card about Happy Holidays, but on the inside of the card I wrote: "Thanks for shaking me up and reminding me of what's important.–Shelly."

I placed it in the pile of cards to friends, cousins, in-laws and teachers and dropped them in the drive through box at the post office. I am not sure what possessed me to do that, but it was very cathartic. I did not tell Jimmy, as he never talks about her and has moved through this better than I.

The Christmas tree we picked out was about the fattest thing on the lot. Grace wasn't sure we would have enough ornaments to put on the chubby tree. Theo laughed and said it reminded him of the way his band director is shaped. At home we put the lights on, but waited until the college boys were back home from college to do the traditional video of the kids putting the ornaments on.

"What do you want for Christmas?" Jim asked me one night.

How do you ask for sincerity, honesty, loyalty, faithfulness, security and undying love and affection? "I dunno," was my lame reply. "Not a purse," I added.

"Yeah, I know."

"Let's just work on the kids first," I offered.

We spent three separate trips shopping together. Yes, together. That is practically a first. In the past we just take a list and shop when we can, in between jobs, swim meets and band concerts, and usually end up with one kid having way too many gifts to open than the others. When we decided to talk over finances with each other recently, we made the decision to involve the other more with financial decisions. It worked! We were finally able to have the first Christmas in years where we did not run credit cards up, and each child had almost the exact same amount of gifts to open. Now granted, shopping with a man is not always right up there with "quality" time, but it was still time spent with *me* and I took it gladly and willingly.

Date nights became less about the bars and bands, and more about new things. We revisited the discount movie theater, tried a new restaurant, and even had our first martini together. Out of all of the years of drinking, neither one of us had ever had a real martini! Well, at $9 a drink, I now know why.

On Christmas Eve we agreed to go to the traditional service at church which was flanked by the family service (little kids singing "Away in a Manger") and the modern service (loud guitars and drums). There were cars everywhere and people coming and going from the various services. Jim doesn't do well in crowds but was an exception to the rule tonight. He warmly greeted everyone who came up to talk to me or the kids. The youth pastor talked the twins collective ears off, and Grace struck up a conversation with a swim team buddy.

At home the twins went off to visit friends in town from their colleges, and Grace put in a Christmas movie. Theo, still obsessed with his birthday Kindle, was reading. Jim took my hand and led me to the tree, now trimmed with all of the ornaments from the last 27 or 28 years of our dating and married lives. He sat me down at the love seat and whispered, "Do you remember our tradition we used to have before the kids came?"

"How could I forget!" I said as I blushed crimson.

When we were young, we used to decorate the tree, shut off all the lights in the house except the tree, then make love in front of it. The colored lights and the rays they gave off with the glow of young love was beyond magical.

"Too risky now," I lamented.

"Maybe not. They have to go to bed sometime," he said, with a twinkle in his eye.

We watched the rest of the movie Grace had put in and saw that the twins were pulling into the drive as we were going upstairs. We finished wrapping a few last-minute items and turned into bed for a long winter's nap.

Sometime around 2 a.m. I was awakened by a handsome man spooning me very close and very tight. I rolled over to face him and he pulled the covers off and said, "The tradition must live on!"

We slipped down the stairs quietly with our big comforter and enjoyed memories from long ago.

One of the nicest things about the kids all being teenaged and older is that no one wakes us up at 5 a.m. anymore. We all seem to sleep in until about 7:30. I needed that after last night's episode under the tree! We ate breakfast before tearing into the gifts.

The kids seemed pleased with their loot, and I was blown away with the gift Jim gave to me. It must be true, the old saying that good things come in small packages. I received a necklace that had six people on it. From left to right, there was a large person, four small people and another large person with the birthstones of Jimmy, the children and me as the head of each of the people. I have seen these on other lovely women and had always though how sweet it was. I never voiced how much I had wanted one, as each charm alone was a small fortune if you get a quality stone.

"Well, did I do good?" Jim wanted to know.

"You did very well, Jimmy."

"I really didn't know what to get you, but you liked the charm bracelet from your birthday."

"You know that all I really need is you. It's all I have ever needed."

"I know."

"Merry Christmas, Jimmy."

"Merry Christmas, Shelly."

I swear I heard Tiny Tim's voice in my head saying: "And God bless us, everyone!"

1 Corinthians 13:4-7
Love is patient, love is kind.
It does not envy, it does not boast, it is not proud.
It is not rude, it is not easily angered,
it keeps no record of wrongs.
Love does not delight in evil but rejoices
with the truth.
It always protects, always truest,
always hopes, always perseveres.

CHAPTER TWENTY-FOUR
Stronger Than Broken

> *"I want somebody who cares for me passionately,*
> *with every thought and with every breath.*
> *Someone who'll help me see things in a different light.*
> *All the things I detest I might almost like."*
>
> **Somebody**
> —Depeche Mode

As the sun came peeking through the purple shades in our bedroom, I felt the prickle of goose bumps rise on my arms. Jim had opened the window a little bit to air out the musty, dusty smell of winter. He does this from time to time during the colder months, just to get some new air into the house. The musty gas heater blowing dusty air into our 60-year-old house seems to make winter drag on and on.

"Hey Shelly. It's not too cold for you is it?" Jim asked.

"No, I need to get up anyway."

I drank my morning glass of water and fired up the treadmill. I dug through the box on the shelf to find the most hard-driving beat for a good sweat and I ran across one of the CDs that got me through those awful days of not eating when I had first found Jim texting Hannah. Do I dare put it on and bring up memories that are working their way further and further into the trash can of my brain? No. Find something techno and get those intervals done quickly.

As I ran the first five-minute warm up, I thought about the mundane things I had to get done later. There was grocery shopping to do, call into work and see what next week's schedule would be for me, get on the computer and transfer the tuition money from our bank to the colleges for the boys, see if Theo's SAT scores were in and so on.

As I completed the intervals I usually do for my winter workouts, I thought about how far Jim and I had come in the last year. Maybe I wasn't going to need the whole year after all. Jim and I can still argue about tuition payments, money issues and how much to spend on each kid at Christmas.

We can dispute about which band to see on a Saturday night or how many hours I should be working to keep us afloat. We can still hurt each other's feelings when we are truthful about what we really want, how we want it or how often we want it. We can still say bone-headed things to each other because we forgot to think before we speak. The difference is, we know in our heart of hearts, that we are the only ones who truly know the other one. We are the only ones who can hold each other up. We can just as easily share our workday, take a run together, watch a show with the kids, enjoy a beer on Saturday night or sit by the fire pit with *our* radio station on.

We work hard at settling arguments quickly, being slow to anger, not using words as weapons, not withholding physical affection when angry and so much more. We learned that compromise is not when both people have to give up something or make concessions. It can be a place where one person reads a whole new page in their lovers life, or where one of us gets a whole new outlook on something we never thought we would like. Once in a while it can feel like "taking one for the team", but that's just it. We are a team. We wear the same jersey and play for the ultimate win. We are in the same boat and have learned to paddle in synchronicity instead of fighting the waves of our own selfish ways.

With God's grace we saved our own marriage. It was not easy. It was genuine work as we prayed, spoke to the pastor, and used some great relationship books to prompt us. It was a struggle to uncover the judgment and blame. It was genuine effort to recommit to each other on paper as well as in our hearts. But we made that choice—together.

Because of God's love we were able to move through this. With our *decision* and *intention* to save this marriage, I don't feel that we will ever intentionally hurt each other, stray or take each other for granted again. I think we will always remember the pain of the last year, but seek to live in the present moment and in the end, we are like the arm I broke when I fell off of my bike when I was 7 or 8 years old.

When I was young, I flipped over my pink bike with the banana seat and the ram's horn handlebars. I threw both arms out as I sailed through the air. The impact was harder on my left arm and I broke the radius and ulna. My mother was so scared at the hospital as the doctor slid the X-ray into his lit screen. He explained to her that this was a common break that was fairly clean. It would heal nicely, he assured her. "In fact," he said, "where the break is will often heal even stronger than before it was broken."

He went on to explain that when the bone breaks, the bone can be set, and where the fracture was will form a mixture of collagen, scar tissue and bone in a sort of matrix around the break, making that particular part of the arm often *stronger* than before. He reminded her that even bone cells are constantly being replaced, renewed and regenerated—and that I would be just fine.

Jimmy's infidelity broke me in two. In many ways Jimmy was broken as well. We stayed together like two pieces of bone ready to join together and heal. And heal we did. We talk openly, we fight less, we make real eye contact, we smile at each other more, we make an effort to include the other one in decisions and we are exploring new and often crazy ways to please each other. We are not perfect, but we are not broken. Yes, that's what Jimmy and I are now...**stronger than broken.**

1 Corinthians 13:13
And now these three remain;
faith, hope and love.
But the greatest of these
is love.

A LETTER FROM JIMMY AFTER READING THIS BOOK:

To my loving wife with her faith and forgiveness,

You did not let a great wrong end our family, which could have been shattered by my selfish act. Through your undying love you somehow saw the big picture to help both of us come back together. Thank you for the love and the faith you had to believe in me.

Jimmy xoxoxoxo

Made in the USA
Charleston, SC
17 September 2015